# Alps mountain biking

# Alps mountain biking

## FROM AOSTA TO ZERMATT: THE BEST SINGLETRACK, ENDURO AND DOWNHILL TRAILS IN THE ALPS

**STEVE MALLETT**

Published by Vertebrate Publishing, Sheffield.
www.v-publishing.co.uk

# Alps
## mountain
### biking

First published in 2015 by Vertebrate Publishing.

 **Vertebrate Publishing**
Crescent House, 228 Psalter Lane, Sheffield, S11 8UT, UK.
www.v-publishing.co.uk

Front cover: Olly Wilkins and Christian Fairclough drop in to the home run up at La Balme in the Chamonix Valley, France.
Photo by Dan Milner. www.danmilner.com.
Back cover: The long descent down the Les Frettes ridge to Le Tour, Chamonix. Photo by Steve Mallett.

A CIP catalogue record for this book is available from the British Library.

ISBN: 978-1-910240-36-6

**VG** Design by Nathan Ryder. Produced by Rod Harrison.
**Vertebrate Graphics Limited**.
www.v-graphics.co.uk

Vertebrate Publishing is committed to printing on paper from sustainable sources.

Printed and bound in Europe on behalf of Latitude Press Ltd.

# Contents

Introduction                                      7
Acknowledgements                                  8
About the guide                                   8
Using the guide                                   9
Grading                                          10
Directions and route planning                    10
Alpine rights of way                             10
Language(s)                                       11
Best type of bike                                11
Kit and spares                                   11
   Food and water                 11
   Tools and spares               11
   Armour and protection          13
   And the rest …                 13
Riding safely                                    13
Mountain rescue                                  13
Area map                                         14

Alpe d'Huez                                      17
Alpi Bike Resort overview                        22
   Bardonecchia                   27
   Sauze d'Oulx                    33

Chamonix overview                                38
   Le Tour and Vallorcine         45
   Les Houches                     51
Crans-Montana                                    57
La Clusaz                                         65
La Grave                                          71
La Plagne                                         75
La Rosière                                        81
La Thuile                                         87
Les Arcs                                          93
Les Deux Alpes                                   99
Les Saisies                                      105
Les Trois Vallées                                111
Leysin                                           117
Martigny                                         123
Megève                                           131
Montgenèvre                                      137
Pila and Aosta                                   143
Portes du Soleil overview                        148
   Les Gets and Morzine           155
   Champéry and Morgins           161
   Châtel and Avoriaz             167

Saint-Luc                                        173
Salève                                           181
Samoëns and the Grand Massif                     187
Serre Chevalier                                  193
Tignes and Val d'Isère                           199
Valloire                                         205
Verbier                                          211
Zermatt                                          219

More riding                                      227
   Aravis                          227
   North-eastern Italy            230
   Northern Alps                  233
   Southern Alps                  239
   Switzerland                    247
   Tour du Mont Blanc             253

Appendix                                         254
About the author                                 255

# Introduction

This is what we all imagine when we picture ourselves riding in the High Alps. You and the machine in perfect harmony, blissfully engaged in a pristine singletrack that picks its way through majestic peaks and valleys and off into the wilds beyond. This of course is a very real possibility, but for many who come to ride in this magnificent region, the reality can be quite different. Instead of this dreamlike scenario, you'll most likely find yourself battling through the tooth-shattering braking bumps of a destroyed bike park, either being held up by a group of fat bankers on their annual trip to Morzine, or being chased down by a gang of horny seasonaires whose rattling steeds clearly receive less of their meagre weekly wage than the local bars.

Fear not though, because with a little bit of planning and research these terrible situations can be avoided, which is where this guidebook comes in.

There is so much more in this central and western area of the Alps than most would lead you to believe, with some of the most stunning enduro and downhill trails you could ever imagine just a ridgeline's hop away from the big and well-publicised resorts. In this book I've attempted to give an overview of the best gravity and lift-assisted riding to be found in this beautiful mountain playground; a wild and awe-inspiring place that holds some of the best trails on the planet – if you're willing to get out there and explore.

There is of course way more riding here than I'm able to explore in this guide, but hopefully it should give you the incentive to look beyond the obvious, away from the crowds and tap into the true potential of the Alps.

◀ High-mountain adventure in Zermatt.

# Acknowledgements

Thanks to Sam and the boys at Bike Village for their advice and guiding in Les Arcs/La Rosière/La Plagne. Finale Freeride for their help with Finale Ligure. Angela Mazzocco at Pila. Nick Maher for advice on the Valais region. Andy Millener for his advice and guiding on the Valais, Martigny, Geneva and beyond. Alex Evans at Châtel bike park. Mark at MTB Verbier for his guidance in Verbier. Martin at Singletrack Safari for his advice with Les Deux Alpes/La Grave. Jamie Carr at Ride the Alps for his input on the Chamonix to Zermatt trips. Janine Imesch at Zermatt. Sylviane Barras at Crans-Montana. The staff at Métabief, Leysin, Dorénaz, Saint-Luc and Megève for all their help and advice in spite of my last-minute organisation. trailAddiction for their advice on the Beaufortain region. Gillon Hunter for his guiding and advice in the southern Alps. My wife Eleanor for keeping me sane at those dark times when trying to deal with ski-resort customer service. Baggen from Alpine Legends for route ideas in the Chamonix valley. Glen Davies and Jamie Barrow for their guidance on riding whilst blind drunk in Chamonix, as well as all the local riders and staff that I've met and ridden with along the way. The chaps at Vertebrate Publishing for all the guidance and to Dave Barter for his efforts in creating the maps.

## About the guide

Two things really struck me during the research for this book. Firstly, the Alps are huge. Secondly, there is not a single piece of a Renault Trafic van that doesn't rattle.

While this latter issue has been solved with some colourful language and the liberal use of a hammer, epic expanses of the Alpine region remain unconquered by most UK riders, and that's where this guide comes in.

By concentrating on the central and western parts of this magnificent landscape, I hope to have given a decent overview of the best places to ride in France, Italy and Switzerland, as well as some route ideas to really get the most out of them. But before you grab the book and go charging off to the mountains, let's just make sure we're on the same page.

I love big descents – it's what the Alps were made for – so for that reason we'll mainly be looking at lift-accessed areas that can really exploit the massive vertical gains to be found. Having said that, I'm not a big fan of fighting my way down the overused main lines of the big bike parks, especially when those winding Alpine singletracks are just a stone's throw away from the crowds.

I hope to show with this guide that you don't necessarily need to trek for days on end to find adventure in the Alps, and even the most popular destinations are home to some spectacular and untouched trails if you're willing to explore a little.

You'll see all the main biking hot spots as well as some areas you've never even heard of and use ski lifts, buses, shuttles, trams and some good old fashioned pedal power to access a wide range of destinations that each offer something a little different. I hope it gives you some new ideas, and the incentive to go out and explore this huge mountain bike playground.

## Using the guide

You should find this guide easy to use. If you know where you want to ride, you'll find all the riding spots listed in alphabetical order, so as long as you can run through A to Z, you're sorted. If you're not sure, or want to plan a tour, check the area map on pages 14–15 to get an idea of where everything is and which spots can be easily linked on a trip.

Once you're on the correct page, you'll find an introduction on what to expect in that area, a look at the riding on offer and three routes that you absolutely have to ride. You'll also find out about the best times to visit, how to get there and where to stay and eat. Useful websites are listed (we've shortened long URLs using tinyurl.com), along with any other information that might be handy.

The opening page for each area contains a quick overview:

An orange bar highlights any area that is particularly good for a given style:

**DOWNHILL**    Lift-accessed DH tracks.

**ENDURO**    Technical downhill riding, some pedalling required.

**SINGLETRACK**    Swooping and flowing singletrack. Expect pedalling.

⬤–⬤  Who's the riding suitable for? See Grading page 10.

🔾  The number of lifts that are available to bikers.

🔽  How much riding time you'll spend descending ...

⬆  ... and pedalling back up.

🕐  The number of days an area is good for.

🧭  How tricky the area is to navigate.

The **maps** give a rough idea of where everything is. Combine them with a trail or IGN (France)/Swisstopo (Switzerland)/IGC (Italy) map to get around, and you'll find what you're looking for. The approximate line of each highlighted route is marked, as are the main towns, roads and peaks.

  You'll find good riding around here.

  Big bike? Head this way for downhill runs.

  If there's a bike park, it's here.

  The approximate line of each of the highlighted routes. Note: line colour does **not** indicate difficulty.

  Lift. Not all accept bikes.

╍╍╍╍  Tram, funicular or mountain railway.

By now the pictures and descriptions should have got you pretty excited and you should have all the information you need to plan a rather good riding holiday. But in case not, there's a 'more riding' section to give you a few ideas. Perhaps you want to visit somewhere new, stop off on the drive to the Alps or go on a big adventure. You'll get some ideas here.

## Grading

Routes in each location are graded blue, red or black in a similar manner to other Vertebrate guides and trail centres around the UK – although it's worth noting that a black-graded Alpine DH is many, many times harder than a black at Coed-y-Brenin. Grades take into account technicality, fitness required, length of trails and gradients. A blue grading means the area can be tackled by most riders. Red locations have riding which is more difficult overall and will only appeal to riders of a good technical and physical ability. A black grading implies very difficult riding for those of an advanced level – you'll find long and sustained descents through remote areas, and routes that require a high skill level to ride.

## Directions and route planning

I've done my best to give accurate directions on how to find the best routes, but this book should never take the place of a map and proper route planning. Where possible we've provided details on the correct map you'll need, or an online resource. If in doubt, hire a guide.

## Alpine rights of way

In general, Europe has a much more relaxed attitude to mountain biking than the UK. The footpath/bridleway setup doesn't really exist, and bikes usually have as much right to roam as anyone else. That said, there are restrictions. Some of the nature reserves and national parks in France and Switzerland do not allow bikes inside and hopefully I've highlighted where you should and shouldn't ride in each area covered.

It's not quite so simple in some areas, such as Chamonix, where mountain bikes are banned from most of the trails during the peak summer season (July and August), but are permitted for the rest of the year. Again I've done my best to cover this, but if you ever encounter signs forbidding the use of mountain bikes then please adhere to them, as it does threaten future use if they are ignored.

As with all paths outside the marked trail centres, always be aware that there may be someone or something around the corner, especially during the peak seasons. Many routes pass through Alpine grazing land and it's not uncommon to find an electric fence placed across a singletrack, or even a cow on the landing of a blind drop. Trust me they don't move, so stay alert.

## Language(s)

Think about learning a few basic sentences – they'll go down pretty well with tourist-weary staff and may get you out of some sticky situations. For this central region, French is a pretty good one to learn, as not only is it good for the French resorts (obviously), but people in both western Switzerland and the many Italian locations close to the French/Swiss border also speak French.

## Best type of bike

This is one of the most talked about issues on forums and magazines when it comes to Alpine riding. I would love to say it doesn't matter, but unfortunately it does. You have to remember that descents in the Alps are sustained and brutal on you and your bike in a way that the UK just isn't. Decent brakes are a must, and full suspension will make the experience much more enjoyable. Above all, make sure whatever you're riding is in good condition. A breakdown or component failure in the middle of the mountains can be very serious indeed, so check your bike over fully before you set off.

Generally speaking, this guide is aimed at the enduro and downhill end of the market, typically a 150- to 180-millimetre travel bike, but of course you can still have fun on a smaller machine.

## Kit and spares

### FOOD AND WATER

Ensure you have a Camelbak-style backpack with at least a litre of water. Even if the route doesn't look strenuous, it's easy to take a wrong turn and be faced with an hour's climb back up to where you began. If you're heading out on longer rides then make sure you pack some energy or cereal bars. Bananas and dried fruits such as apricots are also great options that don't take up too much room.

### TOOLS AND SPARES

Pack a multi tool with a chain splitter, a pump and at least a couple of spare tubes. Pinch punctures are common in this rocky terrain and slices in tyres are not uncommon, so take a tyre boot with you too. Zip ties are ideal for on-the-trail repairs.

You will find small bike-rental shops with a few basic spares, but it's worth remembering that anything specific to your bike will be almost impossible to find in the resorts. Take a spare mech hanger or two, maybe even bolts or linkage parts for the rear suspension if you know they are prone to failing. Other parts such as spokes for a non-standard wheelset will be very hard to locate in the mountain regions, so think hard about what you may need to bring with you. Last but not least, make sure you pack brake pads and check that you have some spare with you for each ride. A set can last as little as one run in some cases!

## ARMOUR AND PROTECTION

A helmet and gloves should be worn at all times, but many riders choose to wear armour, even when they don't usually do so at home. This is by no means essential, but knee pads, full face helmets and back protectors are all worth considering when entering extreme terrain.

## AND THE REST ...

As I said previously, a relevant map is essential, as is a first aid kit, a mobile phone and appropriate clothing. The weather can change fast in the high mountains and altitude can make a huge difference. It may feel warm in the valley, but by the time you arrive at 3,000 metres of altitude – even riding on glaciers in some areas – you can be in bitterly cold conditions. If the weather turns then it can very easily be snowing up high, even in mid summer, so pack a lightweight waterproof no matter what the conditions when you set off. As with anywhere, layers work great, as you can add or remove them as conditions change. Go for synthetic fabrics next to the skin in order to get rid of moisture and keep you warm and dry.

Remember sun cream too. Even if it is cold, you can still get very burned.

## Riding safely

See the **armour and protection** section.

Always let someone know where you're heading each day, especially if you're on your own. If you get into trouble on some of the more remote rides described in this guide, it could be days, or even longer, before anyone finds you. It's also worth riding well within your limits when you're in the back of beyond. It may not be a particularly challenging trail, but the consequences of a crash when you're a long way from civilisation can be serious.

Make sure you have a relevant map and know how to navigate the landscape, especially in poor conditions and visibility.

## Mountain rescue

The emergency number **112** will work in most cases throughout the European Union, with most operators able to speak a good level of English. You will then be directed to the relevant emergency service. It's also worth noting the specific numbers for each country, such as the fire and rescue services:

**France:** 18          **Switzerland:** 118          **Italy:** 115

If possible, be prepared to give a grid reference to your location, as a description may not be enough if you're unfamiliar with the area.

Good insurance cover is also a good idea. Make sure it covers extreme sports and mountain biking as rescue costs, especially by helicopter, can be incredibly expensive.

# Area map

## The main spots

1 Alpe d'Huez ........................... 17
2 Alpi Bike Resort – Bardonecchia ..... 27
3 Alpi Bike Resort – Sauze d'Oulx ...... 33
4 Chamonix – Le Tour and Vallorcine ... 45
5 Chamonix – Les Houches .............. 51
6 Crans-Montana ....................... 57
7 La Clusaz ............................ 65
8 La Grave ............................. 71
9 La Plagne ............................ 75
10 La Rosière .......................... 81
11 La Thuile ........................... 87
12 Les Arcs ............................ 93
13 Les Deux Alpes ...................... 99
14 Les Saisies ......................... 105
15 Les Trois Vallées ................... 111
16 Leysin .............................. 117
17 Martigny ............................ 123
18 Megève .............................. 131
19 Montgenèvre ......................... 137
20 Pila and Aosta ...................... 143
21 PdS – Les Gets and Morzine .......... 155

22 PdS – Champéry and Morgins .......... 161
23 PdS – Châtel and Avoriaz ............ 167
24 Saint-Luc ........................... 173
25 Salève .............................. 181
26 Samoëns and Grand Massif ............ 187
27 Serre Chevalier ..................... 193
28 Tignes and Val d'Isere .............. 199
29 Valloire ............................ 205
30 Verbier ............................. 211
31 Zermatt ............................. 219

### More riding

ARAVIS:
32 Annecy .............................. 227
33 Beaufortain ......................... 229
34 Grand Bornand ....................... 229

NORTH-EASTERN ITALY:
35 Lake Garda .......................... 230
36 Livigno ............................. 231

NORTHERN ALPS:
37 La Bourgeoise ....................... 233
38 La Môle and Les Brasses ............. 233
39 The Jura ............................ 235

SOUTHERN ALPS:
40 Finale Ligure ....................... 241
41 Haute Provence ...................... 243
42 La Moulière ......................... 243
43 Les Terres Noires ................... 244
44 Nice ................................ 244
45 San Remo ............................ 245
46 Sospel .............................. 245

SWITZERLAND:
47 Bex ................................. 247
48 Chamonix to Zermatt ................. 248
49 Eastern Switzerland ................. 249
50 Neuchâtel ........................... 250
51 Rochers de Naye ..................... 250
52 Vercorin ............................ 251
53 Tour du Mont Blanc .................. 253

# Alpe d'Huez

Made world famous by the Megavalanche, Alpe d'Huez has gained something of a celebrity status in the biking community. Huge descents over glaciers, moorland, rocky singletracks and forest trails provide a real variety of terrain in what many claim is the home of modern enduro riding.

## Introduction

Alpe d'Huez sits high on a plateau above Bourg d'Oisans, not far from Les Deux Alpes on the other side of the valley. It's a very different riding experience to the bike park of Deux Alpes though, with the emphasis being on physically challenging natural lines rather than big berms and freeride features.

There are some easy-going DH descents which could be tackled by most, but the majority of the trails are technical, exposed and rocky, so it's no place for beginners or those looking to roll down the mountain in a park environment. To appreciate the good stuff here requires a high level of confidence and fitness, as well as the ability to tackle all sorts of terrain. Navigation is easy enough though, as most trails are marked and don't stray too far from the Alpe d'Huez main face or the Oz valley.

## Trails

Although the trail map looks fairly epic at first glance, you'll notice that everything east of the resort is full-on XC and not really of much interest unless you enjoy slogging up firetracks, which probably isn't why you came to the Alps in the first place. Instead the focus is on the main face above Alpe d'Huez and into the Oz valley.

The main DH lines are to be found off the DMC lift, with a selection of greens through to blacks that cater for most abilities. The best of these is the fast-paced DH track into Oz, but if it's bike park you're after then there are better places. The highlight here is undoubtedly the range of huge enduro descents which are as long and physically demanding as anything you'll encounter on a bike. The most obvious is the spectacular Megavalanche route, which shows off the full range of terrain on offer, beginning over the glacier and taking you through a rocky and barren wilderness before dropping into the woods on fast and switchbacking trails to the valley floor. It's tempting to follow the race run all the way down, but keep your eye out because there many natural and far less ridden singletracks in the woods above Allemont that are well worth exploring. You can catch a bus from here back to Oz.

It's much the same story if you head into the Vaujany valley as well, where the theme is definitely still enduro – the trails littered with rocks, roots and small climbs to keep the height and make the runs as long as possible. It's all genuinely easier to tackle on a trail bike rather than a DH machine so don't be fooled by the big altitude drops, as a heavy rig will limit you to a small area of the mountain.

INTERMEDIATE TO ADVANCED

9

70%

30%

1 WEEK

NOT TOO BAD

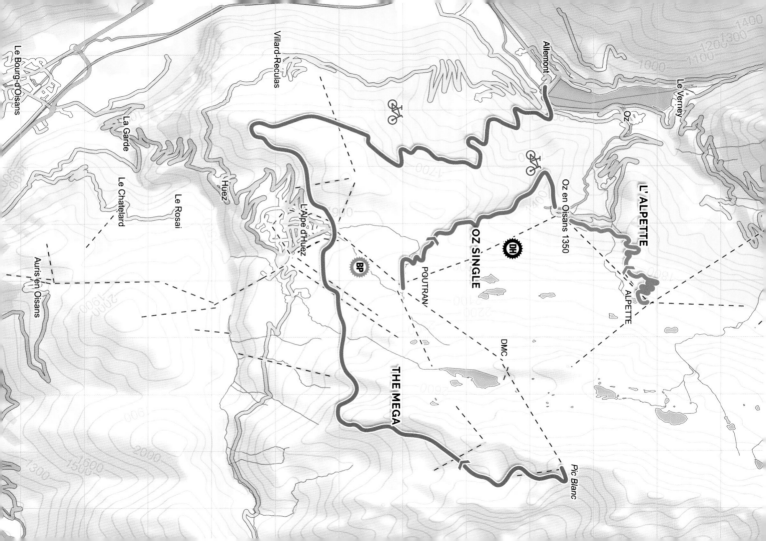

# Alpe d'Huez

## Our Pick

### THE MEGA

Arguably one of the most famous descents on earth, the Megavalanche drops from the highest lift on the hill, the Pic Blanc, right down to Allemont in the Bourg valley. It covers everything from snow to rocky traverses, sandy berms and pine forest switchbacks, with a few wee climbs just to properly finish you off. With over 2,500 metres of altitude drop, you can expect to be frozen solid at the top and lying in a pool of perspiration at the bottom – layers are the way forward here. If you've seen the videos of the race and its mass starts, it can be an eerily quiet experience when riding this run by yourself, but that only adds to the adventure.

### L'ALPETTE TO OZ

From the top of the Alpette lift drop back down the trail towards Oz. Spot a walking trail hooking off to the right. Super technical and rocky at the top, this beautiful singletrack looks as though it may drop towards Vaujany into no man's land. But it's possible to cut back to the Oz lifts where the trail opens up into one of the fastest and most swoopy tracks on the mountain. Totally undiscovered, it's deep in pine needles and a welcome relief from the challenging terrain up top.

## Locals' choice

### OZ SINGLE

A fantastic singletrack option to the main Oz DH run. Off the Poutran 2 or DMC 1 lift, drop into the Oz valley. But instead of heading to the right under the lift, spot the singletrack hugging the left-hand side of the valley. Winding down into the trees it's seemingly never-ending, and your hands will be crying for mercy near the bottom. You'll forget all about that bit on the lift back up though, and eagerly subject yourself to it all over again!

## General info

For all the info on the bike park and lifts, visit tinyurl.com/bike-oisans or www.alpedhueznet.com

For more ideas on routes in the wider area, pick up the free *VTT EN OISANS* guidebook from any of the local tourist infos. It's pretty good and covers just about everything in the area.

## Getting here

The resort can be reached via twenty-one famous Tour de France hairpins above Bourg d'Oisans. If you're not driving down then flying into Grenoble or Chambéry and then renting a hire car is your best bet. It's about 1.5 hours from Grenoble.

# Alpe d'Huez

## Town

Forget any notions of a quaint Alpine village – the ageing high-rise buildings and tacky burger bars up here have about as much charm and character as Butlins. Let's be honest though, on a trip away with mates, most bikers aren't too concerned with culture, and what Alpe d'Huez lacks in that area, it does make up for in nightlife, which is missing in most summer biking resorts. There are many bars and even a nightclub during the peak weeks, so there's plenty of entertainment after the riding's finished.

## Lift dates

Normally the first weekend in July to the last in August but this will probably vary year to year so always check **tinyurl.com/bike-oisans**

## Maps

Bike maps are available from the tourist info in the town centre and at the ticket office at the lifts. You probably won't need anything more detailed, but IGN map *3335 ET: Bourg d'Oisans/L'Alpe d'Huez* covers the area.

## Where to stay

Being a large ski resort that's somewhat empty in the summer, there's a huge amount to choose from. The resort's official accommodation page is a good place to start, with some package deals on accommodation and lift passes: **www.alpedhuez.com**. There are also a number of campsites in the valley beneath Oz.

## Eating and drinking

There's a good number of eateries open during the summer, mostly in the form of burger and snack bars. Head to the Galerie de l'Ours Blanc for some cheap and cheerful grub. Then, having saved so much on dinner, you can splash out the best part of a grand on a bottle of champagne at the Sporting Bar, which has a club open on weekends until 4 a.m.

Also worth checking out is the 'O' Bar. It's slightly out of the way at the bottom end of town but has a real nice atmosphere.

## Bike spares

Sarenne Sports near the main DMC lift has a passable range of spares and rents out Scott and Commençal machines. Rocky Sports, down past the Palais des Sports, also has a decent range of spares.

◄ The notorious Megavalanche route.

# Alpi Bike Resort

overview

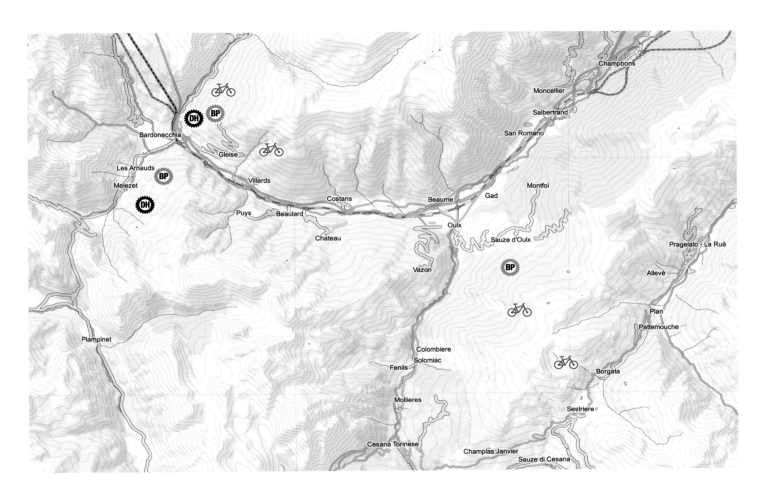

Champbons

Moncellier

Salbertrand

San Romano

Bardonecchia

Gleise

Les Arnauds

Villards

Montfol

Melezet

Costans

Beaume

Gad

Puys

Beaulard

Sauze d'Oulx

Pragelato - La Ruà

Chateau

Oulx

Allevè

Vazon

BP

Plan

Pattemouche

Plampinet

Colombiere

Solomiac

Fenils

Borgata

Mollieres

Sestriere

Cesana Torinese

Champlàs Janvier

Sauze di Cesana

# Alpi Bike Resort overview

The Alpi Bike Resort is a collection of eight towns in the Susa valley region of north-west Italy.

Although each area offers something a little different, they all share a common theme that's typical of the Italian riding scene. You're still very much in the High Alps, but the terrain tends to be gentler than in the French resorts nearby. As a result the trails are long, flowing and easy on the brakes. Rolling through the lush wooded landscape, it's clear that the emphasis is to create fun and swoopy lines that effortlessly carry speed.

Sandy and very dry, the trails have a singletrack and natural feel to them. You won't find anything extreme here, but the local mentality of simply having fun on a bike is utterly contagious. No matter what level you are at, or what you're riding, you'll have a blast in this giant MTB playground.

There are many highlights to the area, such as the national DH course at Sestrière or the enduro wilderness of the Chiomonte valley, but they only offer one or two days of entertainment. Therefore we've chosen to focus on the two riding areas which offer the most longevity and which provide easy access to the smaller resorts in the system: Bardonecchia and Sauze d'Oulx.

## Bardonecchia
At the southern end of the Fréjus Tunnel, this busy town is easily reached from France and receives the largest number of riders in the area.

Infrastructure is great here and the fast lifts give access to a large number of varied trails, from smooth, contouring singletrack to flat-out DH runs. Expect very dry conditions and gentle terrain.

## Sauze d'Oulx
The venue for the Superenduro of Nations, this sunny mountain town is home to some of the best man-made runs you can imagine. You'll swoop, dive and occasionally launch into the bright green forest canopy on these brilliant trails that define the word flow. It's just about possible to link with Sestrière from here too.

## General info
The area has its own website with a general write up on each resort and their locations: tinyurl.com/alpi-bike

## Lift dates
Generally speaking, the lifts run from the end of June through to early September, but each town is slightly different. See the Bardonecchia and Sauze d'Oulx pages for specific dates.

## Getting here
The area is best accessed from Turin, which is an hour away by car, or via Briançon and the Fréjus Tunnel from France: tinyurl.com/alpi-bike-travel

It's also easy enough to get here by train from Turin: www.trenitalia.com

## Where to stay
Bardonecchia and Sauze d'Oulx are the best places to stay as they are easy to reach and have the biggest selections of accommodation and après-bike. See the Bardonecchia and Sauze pages for more information.

◄ Rocce Nera ridge, Sauze.

# Bardonecchia (Alpi Bike Resort)

A welcome relief for any battle-weary biker looking for a chilled cruise around the mountainside. Super-smooth singles wind through the forests, keeping their height and creating wonderful flow. Some properly fast and drifty black runs will keep the adrenaline seeker happy too, so there's something to cater for all tastes and abilities.

## Introduction

Bardonecchia sits on the Italian side of the Fréjus Tunnel. With easy access from both France and the Turin valley, the bike park here is the busiest of all the Alpi Bike resorts. Its popularity also lies in the broad range of riding available. You're likely to see many XC riders mixing it up with full DH rigs, which is testament to the wide appeal of the trails. The swoopy singletracks that criss-cross the southern side of the valley are very much in the style of a UK trail centre – just with a little less rain. You won't find any bogs here, just sandy flowing lines as smooth as silk, along with some kickers and berms built into the black-graded descents. They're not exactly hardcore, but remain great fun for anyone who's tired of having the life battered out of them in the French resorts.

## Trails

The valley can really be split into two zones. The south side is all about the cruisy enduro lines heading back and forth across the mountain. This is where you'll find the majority of riders, piloting all manner of machines along the gently descending singletracks. There are some black- and red-graded trails here too, but they're very easy going indeed and you won't need any more than an all-mountain rig to tackle them. There's some exploring to be done high up on the ridge as well, so it's good to have something you don't mind pedalling.

The eastern side of the valley is definitely the place to head if you're looking for some proper DH action. The Jafferau lift takes you up to 2,000 metres and the descents are steeper as a result. The marked black trails here are still smooth, with little in the way of rocks or roots to hinder your progress, but blimey they're fast. The waves of sand that can be ejected from each corner with a locked-up rear wheel mean there's a lot of pleasure in riding like a total arse. There are also some panoramic backcountry routes to explore from the Jafferau, swinging out into the Rochemolles valley before descending back into the town, or heading out south-east of the spine where natural singletracks weave through the small villages before looping back to the lift station.

It's not easy to ride up to the Jafferau lift station, but there's a linking bus taking riders from the southern side up to the lift station. Therefore it's best to base yourself down in the town or near the Smith lift as you can access the whole area from here without too much slogging along the busy roads.

BEGINNER TO ADVANCED

3

70%

30%

4–5 DAYS

NOT TOO BAD

◄ Give the bike and the body a rest on the smooth Bardonecchia trails.

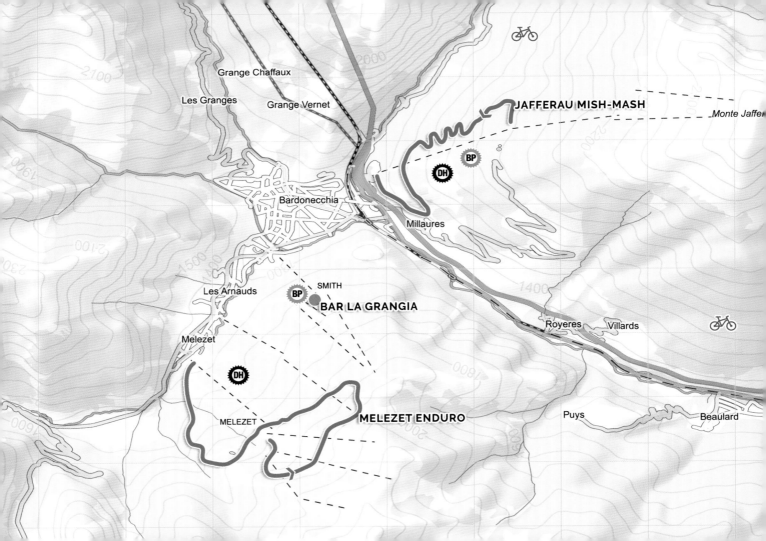

# Bardonecchia (Alpi Bike Resort)

## Our pick

### JAFFERAU MISH-MASH

Follow the signs for the red run off the lift. After descending through a natural gully, hook up with the black trail. This middle section rides incredibly well, with effortless air time guaranteed on the rolling features. Throw some sand off the berms and choke whoever's behind you before heading into the woods on an unmarked trail on the left. This stony singletrack is a total contrast, undulating gently above the motorway, carrying you serenely back to the lift above the chaos below.

### MELEZET ENDURO

A proper XC/enduro loop on a variety of terrain. Climb up the firetrack from the Melezet lift. After twenty minutes you'll see the cows have graciously provided a trail through the trees on the left. Follow this before dropping on to a piste. Take another singletrack contouring left back to the lift and then hook up with the red descent to the valley floor.

## Locals' choice

### BAR LA GRANGIA

Riding is clearly the secondary activity here. If you want to find an Italian on a bike then simply head to this bar/restaurant at the top of the Smith lift. Literally hundreds of bikes are abandoned on the grass in favour of getting smashed and falling asleep on the terrace. This is mountain biking in true Italian style.

## General info

Bardonecchia has a good website with lots of information, pictures and videos of the park: tinyurl.com/bardonecchia-biking

Information on the town and local amenities can be found at tinyurl.com/bardonecchia-info

## Town

The town is a bustling hub for transport between France and Italy via the Fréjus Tunnel. This makes for a lively atmosphere throughout the year and there's no shortage of bars, restaurants and shops to choose from. At first glance the valley appears quite industrial and clearly a lot of trade takes place here. This is still a major ski resort though and the centre retains a lot of pretty, chalet-style architecture. Big mountain views all around leave no doubt that you're in the heart of the High Alps either, and provide an epic backdrop.

## Getting here

Access is easy enough if you're driving from France. The town is right at the end of the Fréjus Tunnel, around 120 kilometres from Chambéry (1.5 hours by car). From Turin airport it's only 1 hour by car or by train: www.trenitalia.com

# Bardonecchia (Alpi Bike Resort)

## Lift dates

From July to early September: tinyurl.com/bardonecchia-lifts

## Maps

A map can be obtained from any of the lifts or online: tinyurl.com/bardonecchia-map

The area is also covered by an Italian IGC 1:25,000 map: Sheet 104: *Bardonecchia/Monte Thabor/Sauze d'Oulx.*

## Where to stay

Camping Bokki and Camping Pian del Colle are both ideally located for the Melezet lift. There's a huge selection of apartments, hotels and bed and breakfasts in the town. Most can be found on the official site: tinyurl.com/bardonecchia-info

## Eating and drinking

There's a lot of choice here and a nice mix of French and Italian dishes. On the mountain, head to La Grangia and talk nonsense with the locals over a beer and a burger. Back in town a good choice is Lo Chalet Bardonecchia. It's not cheap but the food is outstanding.

Café Medail is a café/bar located on the corner of the main street and is a great place to chill and people-watch.

## Bike spares

The park is officially sponsored by Kona and you'll find hire bikes at the bottom of the Smith lift. Rent and Go and Calzati Bike are also located in the Smith lift area and have some basic spares in stock.

# Sauze d'Oulx (Alpi Bike Resort)

Although not a huge riding area, the bike park at Sauze d'Oulx near the French/Italian border is one of the best in the central Alps. Clever use of the mellow terrain gives all the trails here a flowing and natural feel that all abilities will find incredibly addictive.

## Introduction

Sauze d'Oulx is perhaps the best known of the eight Alpi Bike resorts in Italy. This is largely due to the town hosting the Superenduro of Nations, but also because the trails here have notoriously become great fun to ride. It's genuinely one of the few destinations where it's not necessary to explore out of the park – the marked runs really are that good.

Any level of rider on pretty much any machine will feel something verging on ecstasy as they float and dive through the rollercoaster features of this gentle mountainside. All the trails follow the same basic recipe of fun rather than extreme, and while big, rolling tabletops and north shore hits have been built into some of the runs, they have a grin factor rather than terror aspect to them. The sandy terrain means braking bumps don't form easily here and most of the trails remain smooth and fast throughout the season.

## Trails

Navigating your way around the hillside isn't too difficult, but finding your way to the lift most certainly is. You actually need to head below the main town to the hamlet of Jouvenceaux. From here you should be able to follow someone down the small streets to the lift, where the staff will happily give you a ski map in order to find the trails. This is less than useless, but luckily the runs are marked well once you're off the lift and as you cruise along the firetrack you'll see most of them dropping off to the left at regular intervals.

It's in this undulating woodland that most of the riding takes place and you'll soon notice that there are sandy flowing lines almost everywhere. Like yellow ribbons in the luscious forest floor, the trails glide effortlessly over crests and through natural gullies, giving an almost weightless sensation. The second lift takes you up above the tree line to the Rocce Nera where things get even better. The views up here are sensational, but you won't care. All focus is on the magnificent gorse-lined singletrack that rolls even better than the stuff in the woods. There may not be many lines, but the feeling of rising and falling at warp speed through this spectacular landscape never gets old. Unfortunately this top lift is only open on certain weekends, but if you're armed with an enduro machine – which is ideal here – then it's not a bad climb from the first lift and you'll have these beauties all to yourself.

There is scope for some exploring. Climbing from the Rocce Nera lift it's possible to make some big loops over the ridge into the Sestrière valley and return via the Fraiteve cable car. Is it worth it though when the marked trails here are so good?

BEGINNER TO ADVANCED

2

80%

20%

1 WEEK

NOT TOO BAD

◄ Swooping through the Sauze forest.

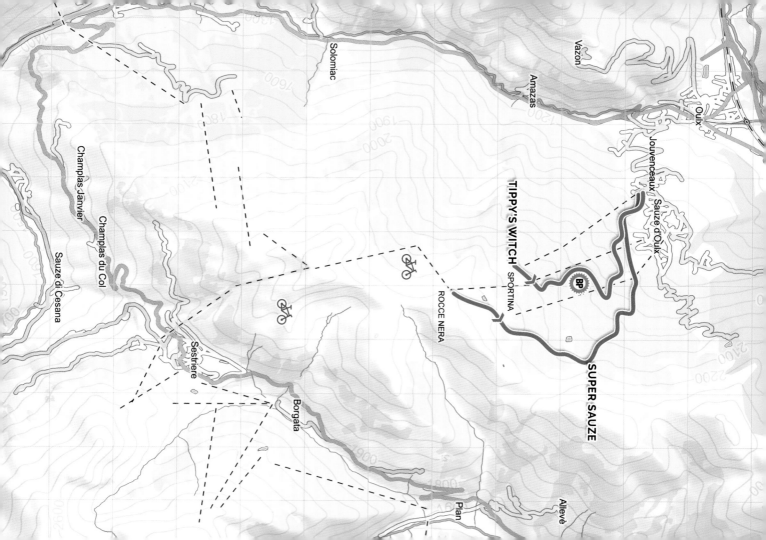

# Sauze d'Oulx (Alpi Bike Resort)

## Our pick
### SUPER SAUZE
From the top of the Rocce Nera lift, follow the signs for the No 12 or Super Sauze trail. You may find yourself climbing up if the lift isn't running, but trust me – it's worth it. A glorious blast along open and undulating terrain launches you into the woods along a sort of freeride singletrack with wooden hits in all the right places. One of the most fun lines you'll ever ride.

### TIPPY'S WITCH
This red-graded run is the most bike park style run here, but it's a long way off the destroyed and lumpy mess you might expect. Long, rolling tabletop jumps give even more of that floating feeling, while exaggerated natural crests get you properly airborne. Without any steep sections or tight corners the trail remains in great condition, as it's rare that you need to get hard on the brakes.

## Locals' choice
### EVERYTHING
The mountain has a chilled vibe and it's not uncommon to see groups of mates on hardtails and V10s riding the same lines together. They simply love being on bikes and it's an infectious mentality that makes every trail here a total blast no matter what your level or preferred riding style.

## General info
The best source for information is the Sauze Freeride site, which has lift dates, photos and a passable trail map: **www.sauzefreeride.net**

Information on the area in general can be found at: **www.sauzeonline.com/summer**

## Getting here
The town isn't far from Bardonecchia and the Fréjus Tunnel, so boasts easy access from both France and Italy. The closest airport is Turin which is around 1 hour by car. It's also an easy journey by train from Turin to Oulx, from where you can catch a bus to Sauze d'Oulx. Information on this and airport transfers can be found here: **www.sauzeonline.com/travelling-to-sauze**

# Sauze d'Oulx (Alpi Bike Resort)

## Town

Part of the Via Lattea system that links the town with Sestrière, Sauze d'Oulx is clearly a ski resort, with many high-rise apartment blocks. It's still a pleasant spot though and retains a lively atmosphere throughout the summer months. There's no shortage of bars and restaurants here and most are English speaking. With a real chilled Italian vibe and plenty of top-notch street food to snack on, the town is a great place to wind down after a good day's riding, taking in the dying rays over the lush valleys below.

## Lift dates

From the end of June to early September: tinyurl.com/sauze-lifts

## Maps

A map can be obtained online: tinyurl.com/sauze-maps

You'll probably not need it, but if you want a 'proper' map, try the Italian IGC 1:25,000 sheet 104: *Bardonecchia/Monte Thabor/Sauze d'Oulx*.

## Where to stay

With many ski apartments and hotels to choose from you should be able to find suitable accommodation here. Hotel Gran Baita is popular among bikers. A good range of options can also be found here: www.sauzeonline.com/accommodation

## Eating and drinking

Although the town isn't particularly big, it remains busy throughout the year and is very popular with the Turin crowd. Food and drink is a top priority here and there's something for all tastes and budgets. L'Assietta is a popular central hangout and serves great pizza and beer. Paddy McGinty's Irish pub is also a good option for the obligatory pizza and beer and often has live music in the evenings. Try Del Falco restaurant for some proper Italian fine dining.

## Bike spares

There aren't too many options here but Faure Sport in the centre is a good option with Kona hire bikes, armour and some basic spares on offer.

◄ North shore hip/drop. Sauze bike park.

Chamonix
overview

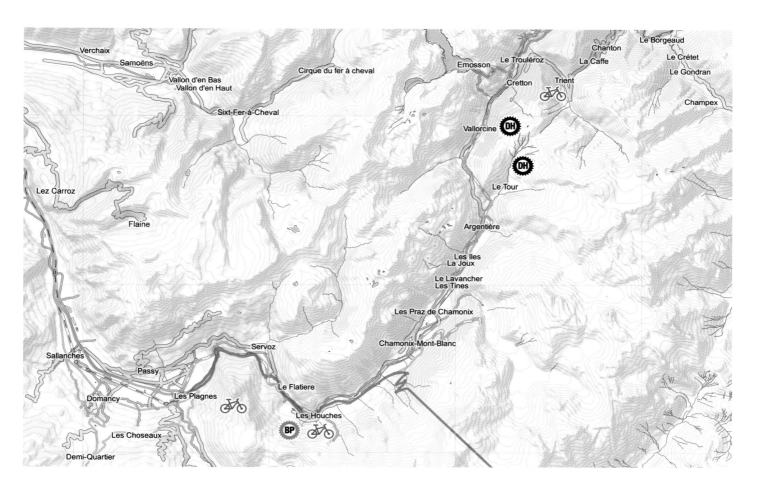

Verchaix

Samoëns

Vallon d'en Bas
Vallon d'en Haut

Cirque du fer à cheval

Emosson

Le Trouléroz

Chanton

Le Borgeaud

La Caffe

Le Crétet

Cretton

Trient

Le Gondran

Sixt-Fer-à-Cheval

Champex

Vallorcine

**DH**

Lez Carroz

**DH**

Le Tour

Flaine

Argentière

Les Iles
La Joux

Le Lavancher
Les Tines

Les Praz de Chamonix

Servoz

Chamonix-Mont-Blanc

Sallanches

Passy

Le Flatiere

Domancy

Les Plagnes

Les Houches

Demi-Quartier

Les Choseaux

**BP**

# Chamonix overview

The Chamonix valley is nothing short of stunning. Simply nowhere else in the Alps has terrain, scenery or a reputation that can match it. Famous as the gateway to the mighty Mont Blanc, climbers, hikers and busloads of irritating tour groups are drawn from all over the world to the original home of alpine sports.

The town sits on the valley floor, dominated by the gigantic peaks and glaciers all around. It's no hidden mountain retreat though and is buzzing throughout the year, with plenty of bars and clubs offering way more après-bike than any other mountain resort in the summer. When it comes to food it gets even better. Only the big cities can match what's on offer here and even the most awkward cravings are covered. Some decent bike shops ensure there are many hire and mechanical support options available as well.

Surprisingly Chamonix itself doesn't offer the best riding. The main reason for this is the sheer number of walkers on the trails, with resulting restrictions and threats of fines everywhere in the summer season. The other problem is that the valley is incredibly steep and most of it is genuinely not great on a bike anyway.

Your only real option is off the Brévent lift. Local boy Baggen from Alpine Legends suggests heading west down the ridge towards Aiguillette des Houches and then dropping down to Les Houches town. This panoramic and technical line is a beauty, but expect a foul-mouthed tirade if you tackle it during peak season.

For these reasons we've focused our guide on the neighbouring towns of Le Tour and Les Houches. Positioned at each end of the valley, these offer some truly spectacular riding away from the crowds where the terrain is far less severe. It's possible to base yourself in Chamonix town and access these areas by car or a short train ride, so you get the best of both worlds.

## Le Tour and Vallorcine

Le Tour is at the northern end of the Chamonix valley, on the Swiss border. The smooth and flowing trails here are some of the best high mountain singletracks you'll find anywhere in the world, while the vivid glaciers and jagged ridgelines that surround Le Tour ensure that this is a very special place to ride indeed.

## Les Houches

At the south-western end of the valley sits Les Houches. Often overlooked and forgotten by the world of mountain biking, this wooded hillside is home to a network of fun, technical singletracks. A new bike park was added for 2013 so there's a good variety of riding here.

◄ Focusing on the trail, not the view of Mont Blanc from Le Tour.

CHAMONIX – OVERVIEW    41

# Chamonix overview

## General info

There's not too much information on the riding in the area and that's generally because bikes aren't encouraged around Chamonix. However some local chaps have put together a great blog and the book can be bought online. Everything from trails to bus timetables: www.thechamonixbikebook.com

Although some information is out of date, another good source for route ideas is tinyurl.com/chamonix-biking

## Getting here

Chamonix is around 1.5 hours from Geneva by car. Transfers can be booked through ChamExpress: **www.chamexpress.com**

It's also possible to get a train from Geneva, although it is a little complicated. All the info is at **tinyurl.com/chamonix-travel**

## Lift dates

See Le Tour and Les Houches (pages 45 and 51).

## Where to stay

There's no shortage of accommodation in Chamonix, although it can be pricey compared to other resorts. Most options can be found here: tinyurl.com/chamonix-accommodation

For a more budget option there are campsites in and around the Chamonix area: **tinyurl.com/chamonix-camping**

## Eating and drinking

There's simply too much to list here but the micro brewery MBC is an absolute must, serving up delicious home brews and legendary burgers.

Also check out local favourite Le Vert at the southern end of town, which has a fancy selection of international cuisine with live music often playing in the bar area.

Bars and clubs are everywhere in Chamonix. A local favourite is Bar'd Up, which often has live music and a chilled atmosphere.

Afterwards head to L'Amnesia nightclub where the night usually ends up pretty messy. Don't expect to be doing much riding the next day.

## Bike spares

One of the best options is Chamonix Bike Rental, which offer Nukeproof machines to rent and a workshop you can use yourself: www.chamonixbikerental.com

Zero G has a decent range of rental bikes, spares and clothing available. Uber flash in typical Chamonix style, it's also good for a bit of bike porn window shopping as well: **www.zerogchx.com**

# Le Tour and Vallorcine (Chamonix)

Probably the best riding in the Chamonix valley and quite possibly the entire world, Le Tour and the adjoining Vallorcine valley boast some legendary trails. Add in breathtaking scenery wherever you look and you've got backcountry blasting at its absolute finest.

## Introduction

Le Tour sits at the Swiss end of the valley and has by far the gentlest terrain in the area (by Chamonix standards at least). It's way more bike friendly as a result and finally gives you a chance to let off the brakes. All the good stuff requires a small push or pedal to access, but it's all easy enough to find if you're armed with a map. What the map won't tell you is just how perfect the trails are. Every ridgeline is topped with a ribbon of gorse-lined singletrack winding off towards the vivid blue glaciers and immense peaks. The bike park here is pretty good too and receives so few riders that the descents are in great condition. The few north shore sections built in add some decent variety when mixed in with the natural stuff. There's plenty more in the Vallorcine valley as well, so more than enough to keep you entertained for a week.

## Trails

Much of the good stuff is to be found above Le Tour, where the terrain is far less severe than the vertical faces either side of Chamonix. Set amongst the gnarliest terrain in the Alps, it's a surprise to find yourself totally flat out on tarmac-smooth singletrack, sweeping through the gorse and heather. There are of course many technical sections around, especially on the high ridges and in the tight switchbacks of the forest lower down. But it's this variety that focuses the mind like nowhere else and leaves you gagging for more. Every trail feels better than the last and seems to go on forever. We often found ourselves giggling, euphoric and sometimes even a little angry at just how good

the last descent was. It really is amazing stuff, and you'd be a fool not to come here ... I'm getting angry again.

Most of the riding takes place above the tree line, where the terrain feels very much like moorland. Shaley but extremely hard-packed, most of these trails drain very well indeed and can be dusty within a day or so of heavy rain. They're also quite easy to find, dropping along two ridgelines back into the Cham. valley, or off the Col de Balme into Vallorcine. If you're after a little more adventure it's possible to drop way down into Trient and Martigny, and get the train back to Cham. or the bus to the Col des Montets. But you'll definitely want a good map for that.

So what's the downside? Well the descents can be a bit too long I suppose and the glaciers can be a little dazzling in direct sunshine.

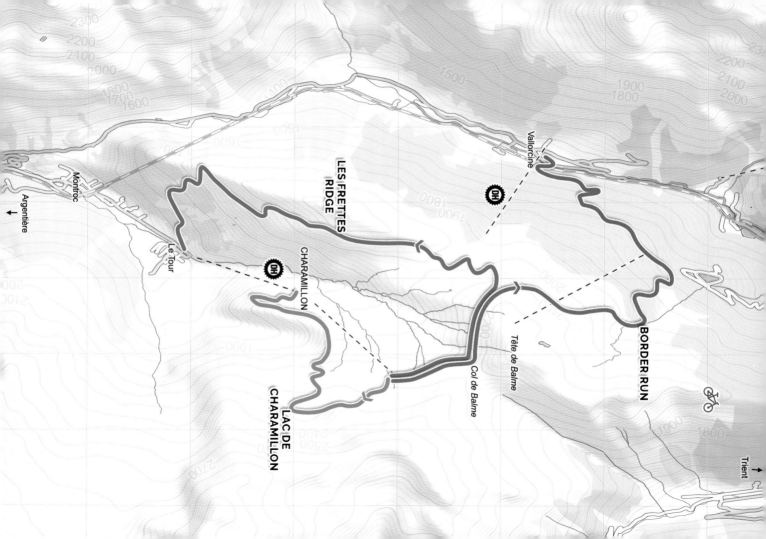

# Le Tour and Vallorcine (Chamonix)

## Our pick
### BORDER RUN
This fast and snaking trail really is the epitome of high Alpine riding. From the top Charamillon chairlift, traverse to the Col de Balme and continue under the Tête de Balme. Rather than dropping left to the Col des Posettes, take a right along a roller coaster singletrack into Switzerland which is nothing short of breathtaking. Take the left-hand option at every junction to meet up with a large firetrack and winter ski piste. Follow this until the first right-hand hairpin where you'll spot a sweet woodland path to the left. Cut straight across the firetrack at the bottom to hook up with the brilliant and long-forgotten Vallorcine DH track. Even the most militant bike park haters will be bowled over by the steep rocky turns and swoopy drops which take you all the way to Vallorcine, where you can take the lift back up to the Col des Posettes.

### LAC DE CHARAMILLON
From the top Charamillon chairlift at Le Tour, take a right and climb up the trail you can see cutting across the steep face in front of you. Shortly after the Lac de Charamillon, drop to the right and make sure you've got a camera for this beautiful ridgeline that hugs the side of the Vormaine combe. But for heaven's sake cut back to the lift when you're opposite it, as carrying too far along the ridge results in a world of pain (I know).

## Locals' choice
### LES FRETTES RIDGE
From the Col de Balme drop down a magnificent hardpack run to the Col des Posettes. From here traverse around the left of the Aiguillette des Posettes until you reach a crossroads. Either drop to the left for a brilliant flowing trail across the face or head up to the ridgeline which is super technical and almost trials-like in sections. Either trail finishes in the woods above the Col des Montets, which is more fun than I can possibly describe with seemingly endless switchbacks back into Le Tour. Be aware though that this area is forbidden to bikes during July and August and if you attempt it during this period you're likely to be killed by loopy camera-toting tourists.

## General info
There's not too much information around on the area and that's generally because bikes aren't encouraged around Chamonix. But some local chaps have put together a great blog and the book can be bought online. Everything from trails to bus timetables can be found at:
www.thechamonixbikebook.com
Also check: tinyurl.com/chamonix-biking

## Getting here
From Chamonix it's a 10-minute drive to Le Tour. Alternatively it's a cheap journey by train to Montroc or Vallorcine.

# Le Tour and Vallorcine (Chamonix)

## Town

Although both occupy beautiful settings, neither Vallorcine or Le Tour has a lot to offer in the summer months. It's a far better bet to stay in Chamonix itself and then make the small drive to Le Tour. If you're without transport then it's possible to get the train to Montroc and then cycle up the hill to the lift. Argentière is also worth considering if you're around during the peak weeks and find that Chamonix is packed out. It has a few bars in the evening and it's not too far to cycle to the Charamillon télécabine at Le Tour.

## Lift dates

Like most of the Chamonix valley, Le Tour benefits from a long season, with the lifts running from June until the end of September. Dates and times can be found at **www.chamonix.com**

## Maps

A map can be obtained from the lift caisse at Le Tour or Vallorcine which shows you all of the two or three MTB trails in the Chamonix valley ... A better bet is the Chamonix IGN map (*3630 OT: Chamonix*) or just winging it.

## Where to stay

Best to stay in Chamonix and take advantage of the great nightlife there. There are plenty of hotels and apartments but they can be pricey. Most options can be found at: **tinyurl.com/chamonix-accommodation**

There are campsites in and around the Chamonix area: **tinyurl.com/chamonix-camping**

## Eating and drinking

At Le Tour itself you're likely to starve to death, or have your pants pulled down by the extortionate restaurant at the bottom of the télécabine. The refuge at the Col de Balme just after the Col des Posettes is about the best place during the day, with beautiful views over the Glacier du Tour. In the evening head to Cham. and gorge yourself (see page 43).

## Bike spares

Again you'll need to head to Chamonix town for this. Check out the Chamonix overview, page 43.

# Les Houches (Chamonix)

Les Houches sits at the southern end of the Chamonix valley and is home to some outstanding backcountry singletrack. Often overlooked as a biking destination, there are far fewer riding restrictions than in Chamonix itself, so you're free to explore this enduro heaven. The views of Mont Blanc, which looms overhead, aren't too shabby either.

## Introduction

The recent history of biking in Les Houches has been somewhat erratic. A massive investment a few years ago went into a decent bike park which was soon dismantled and moved to the other side of the mountain. The future of the current park is just as unsure due in no small part to the pressures of hikers in the area. However, the best thing about Les Houches is, and always was, the unmarked singletrack hidden in the woods. Hard-packed and rocky with not a whole lot of pedalling, these trails are quite simply brilliant on anything from a hardtail to a full DH rig. They really are one of the best-kept secrets around and, like the rest of the valley, the scenery is out of this world. The trails are long too, meaning you could happily spend a few days exploring this forgotten mountain.

## Trails

Les Houches has never received a lot of press, being completely overshadowed by Chamonix and Mont Blanc both figuratively and literally — it's little more than a random hill at the south-western end of the famous ridgeline. It has some great riding though, something that was finally realised by the town when they built the original park under the Bellevue lift. Officially the park is no more, but the trails are still there, forgotten but still just as good with a wonderful flow. With no one riding them, they've taken on a singletrack nature, yet are heavily bermed with sections of rollers. It's quite unique actually. Heading west across the hillside, you'll drop away from the plateau, with its sensational glacier backdrop, and into the woods, where the

real draw of Les Houches lies hidden. There's a huge network of natural trails in here that switchback down into the valley. Packed with fun features courtesy of Mother Nature, the trails are hardpack and can be incredibly smooth in certain sections, making it very fast rolling indeed. You have to be careful not to get too carried away or you'll be hitting sprawling root sections at ludicrous speeds. Conveniently the trails all lead back into the town for another round. The Prarion lift gives direct access to the new park, which essentially consists of variations of a single run. It's good stuff though with plenty of berms and rollers through loamy terrain that's suitable for most abilities.

There's also scope for big days out using the tramway from Saint-Gervais further down the valley. It takes a brave man to descend down there though as a lift back up is at the driver's discretion — and if he's in a bad mood you've got a long climb back up the road.

| | INTERMEDIATE TO ADVANCED |
|---|---|
| ⓐ | 2 |
| ⬇ | 70% |
| ⬆ | 30% |
| 🕐 | 2–3 DAYS |
| ⊘ | NOT TOO BAD |

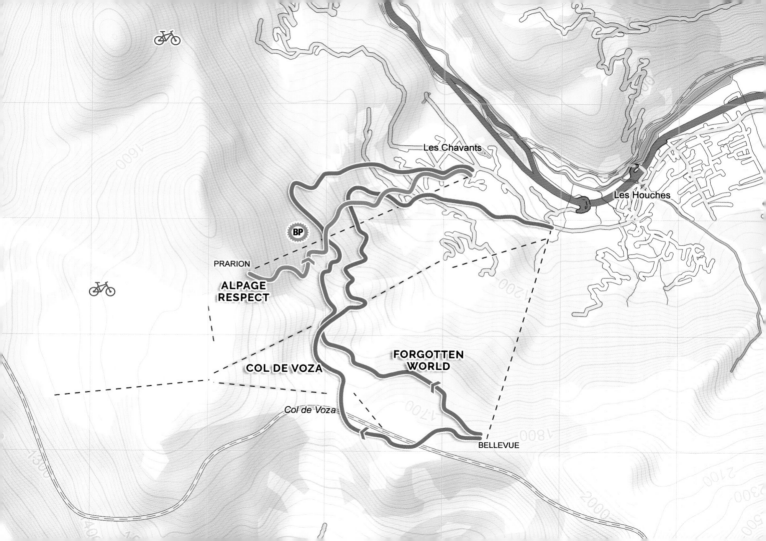

Les Chavants

Les Houches

BP

PRARION

**ALPAGE
RESPECT**

**COL DE VOZA**

**FORGOTTEN
WORLD**

Col de Voza

BELLEVUE

# Les Houches (Chamonix)

## Our pick
### FORGOTTEN WORLD
Head right out of the Bellevue lift and keep your eyes peeled for a trail in the bushes on the right. This may not look promising but you're soon hammering along an existing run. You'll need to peel off this roller coaster at the second set of switchbacks to pick up a firetrack. After 500 metres, head left behind a restaurant to find yourself on a fast, swoopy and endless singletrack that gradually winds its way into Les Chavants. Follow the walking signs back to the Prarion lift.

### COL DE VOZA
Another enduro loop. Follow the signs for the Col de Voza from the Bellevue lift along a ridgeline trail. At the col spot the trail through the grass heading back in to the valley. Picking up the same firetrack as above, continue a little further this time to see a narrow trail on the left. This one clings to the hillside and can be quite technical in places but is no less fun. Instead of dropping into Les Chavants, climb the road a little to pick up another singletrack all the way into the centre.

## Locals' choice
### ALPAGE RESPECT
The local chaps are keen to push their new blue run new from the Prarion lift. Although clearly no good at naming trails they do know how to build them. It's one of those lines that really does have something for everyone, with plenty of rolling features allowing you to cruise or go ballistic. It reminds you how good a man-made trail can be when huge numbers aren't riding them.

## General info
The official Les Houches site has a small amount of general info:
**www.leshouches.com**

A little better is the general Chamonix guide:
**tinyurl.com/chamonix-biking**

## Getting here
Coming from Geneva it's around 1.5 hours to Les Houches and a further 10-minute drive to Chamonix.

It's possible to take a train from Geneva via Annemasse, which takes about 2 hours 15 minutes: **tinyurl.com/chamonix-travel**

A minibus transfer can be booked through ChamExpress:
**www.chamexpress.com**

# Les Houches (Chamonix)

## Town

Although part of the same ski system, Les Houches is no party venue like Chamonix. Primarily a small town rather than a ski resort, it has a laid-back feel with not a whole lot going on in the summer. But being the start to many hikers' ascents of Mont Blanc via the Bellevue gondola, it's not exactly dead either and there are plenty of worse places to stay for a few days. Chamonix is after all only 10 minutes up the road via car or the train, so Les Houches is a good alternative with cheaper accommodation available, especially in the summer months.

## Lift dates

Like most of the Chamonix valley, Les Houches benefits from a long season with the Bellevue lift running from May into October. Dates and times can be found at **www.chamonix.com**

## Maps

A very basic map can be obtained from the lift caisse at the Bellevue or Prarion lifts. Again an IGN map is highly recommended, in this case *3531 ET: Saint-Gervais-Les-Bains.*

## Where to stay

As with the rest of the valley it's best to stay in Chamonix and take advantage of the great night life there. There are plenty of hotels and apartments but they can be pricey. Most options can be found at: **tinyurl.com/chamonix-accommodation**

For a cheaper option there are campsites in and around the Chamonix area: **tinyurl.com/chamonix-camping**

## Eating and drinking

During the day a limp and pitiful sandwich can be had opposite the Bellevue lift at Le Spot. If you're feeling flush head for Le Basilic which serves top quality grub: **tinyurl.com/topqualitygrub**

In the evening head to Cham. and party (see the Chamonix overview, page 43).

## Bike spares

Again you'll need to head to Chamonix town for this. Check out the Chamonix overview, page 43.

# Crans-Montana

The quality DH runs at Crans-Montana are a huge draw for those who enjoy a smooth, roller coaster blast down a mountain. But don't write the area off as nothing more than a small bike park, as the huge height gains and breath-taking scenery make this a quality venue for some epic gravity-assisted adventure.

## Introduction

The mountain resorts of Crans and Montana in the eastern Valais have joined forces to create an uber posh venue in which to buy chocolate and cuckoo clocks. There's a lot of cash kicking around and it shows in the two downhill tracks above the village, which are some of the finest man-made runs you'll ever encounter. It's easy to see why most riders who visit are happy to session the park on full DH rigs – but it's a bit of a shame when that's all they do, because the high-altitude enduro routes here are world class, providing monstrous descents of almost 2,500 vertical metres, right down to the valley floor. They won't be of much interest to beginners, but for those with strong technical ability, these challenging backcountry trails that drop over glaciers, down rocky spines, and through woodland and vineyards will be very hard to beat for that all important 'out there' feel.

Arm yourself with a big-travel trail bike and you've got just about everything covered here.

## Trails

Three lifts operate from Crans-Montana; the Cry d'Er, the Violettes and the Plaine Morte télécabines. The Cry d'Er is of most interest to riders making a day trip here, as it serves the brilliantly designed bike park trails. There are only two runs, effectively an intermediate and a hard option, but both offer some fantastic flow and use the gently rolling slopes to full swoopy effect. The red run in particular is a classic, carrying flat-out speed through the long sweeping turns that catapult you beautifully into every sweet jump along the way.

Anyone of an intermediate level upwards will have a blast in the park, but really it's only good for a couple of days before you're eager to explore further, and that's where the Plaine Morte cable car comes in, which roughly translates as 'total death'.

With a top station at nearly 3,000 metres in altitude, the views over the glacier and the peaks beyond are incredible, as are the dark ribbons of steep and snaking singletrack that cut through the shale of the barren terrain below. It's tricky stuff for sure and quite scary at times due to the huge drops next to trail, but this is riding at the most epic of epicness, especially if you drop right down to the valley bottom via the Tseuzier Dam, which is pretty much a day out in itself. A funicular running from Sierre back up to the resort makes this huge run possible with minimum pedal time, but don't underestimate just how full on these long and demanding loops can be.

Which bike you bring along depends largely on the time of year. There's a long season here, but outside July and August you're limited to the Cry d'Er lift which, unless you fancy a grim slog up the mountain, only gives access to the park, so you might as well bring a big rig and enjoy some no-nonsense DH action during the autumn period.

**ENDURO/DOWNHILL**

| | |
|---|---|
|  | INTERMEDIATE TO ADVANCED |
|  | 3 |
|  | 70% |
|  | 30% |
|  | 4–5 DAYS |
|  | NOT TOO BAD |

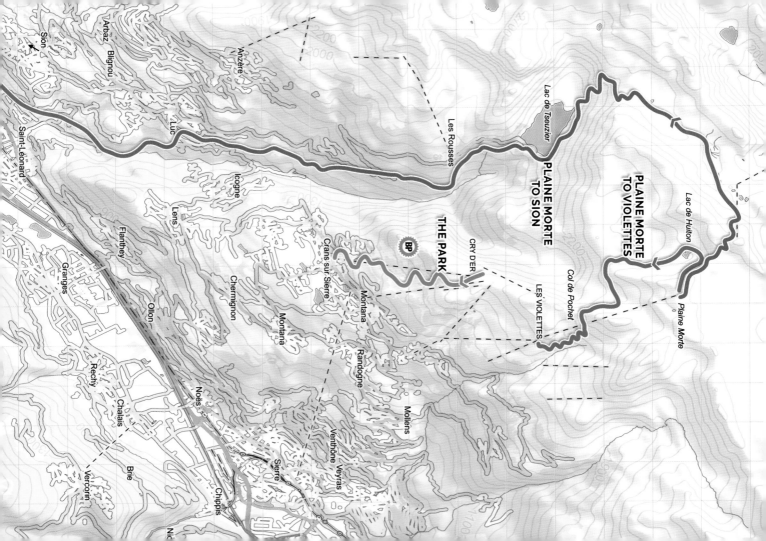

# Crans-Montana

## Our pick
### PLAINE MORTE TO VIOLETTES

Take a series of lifts out of Montana up to the Plaine Morte, where you'll be greeted by staggering views over the glacier below. Take a left and climb briefly to the peak before dropping down the ridgeline and drifting through the shale towards the col ahead of you. As the trail levels out, head to the left into a second valley following signs for Lac de Huiton. The mellow gradient through this valley means you can really rip and carve through the hardpack and shale singletrack, while smooth rock slabs work as God's hand-made kickers. Keep heading left around the spine following signs for Crans-Montana and Violettes. Push up to the Col de Pochet and then glide back down to the Violettes along glorious singletrack through the meadows.

### PLAINE MORTE TO SION

The big one. Initially, follow the Violettes route above, but instead of heading left to the Lac de Huiton, push up to the col beneath the Wisshore and then drop straight over the back following signs for the Col du Rawil. This section is absolutely fantastic, taking you into the middle of nowhere through a wild switchback feast. Things get less extreme but no less beautiful as you traverse along a smooth singletrack plateau and through a rocky tunnel which brings you out on to the slopes above the iridescent Lac de Tseuzier. The trail gets extremely exposed and terrifying as you drop from the lake towards Produssex (which roughly translates as 'sexual produce'), but mercifully becomes easier going as you criss-cross the main road on a mixture of double and singletrack, following signs to Luc. There's one last piece of awesomeness as you dive through the gorge between Luc and Saint-Léonard and out into the vineyards above Sion. Find your way to the station for a ride back to Sierre, where you can take the funicular up to Crans-Montana.

## Locals' choice
### THE PARK

There may be only two runs to choose from here, but the mellow and varied terrain makes for a toboggan-style run of rapid insanity. The jumps on both descents are exceptionally well designed so that while timid riders can crawl over them, the more experienced can treat them like interstellar launch pads. Riders from all over the Alps make the long drive here for an afternoon of ego-boosting trails that make you feel like a proper pro. Both runs finish with a north shore section and some hefty drops straight into the car park, where you can grab a beer in the bar and reflect on just how awesome you are.

# Crans-Montana

## General info

The official tourism site is great, with plenty of info on the park trails, opening dates and on the area in general: **www.crans-montana.ch/ete**

It's also worth searching out their Facebook page for any updates on special offers, events or lift closures.

## Getting here

Crans-Montana sits at a 1,500-metre altitude on a picturesque plateau above Sierre in the eastern Valais region of Switzerland. You can catch the train from Geneva to Sierre which takes around 2 hours, and then the funicular up to Crans-Montana. You can book train tickets here: **www.sbb.ch**

If you have your own transport then you can reach the resort in 1.5 hours from Chamonix. You'll also be able to access other nearby areas such as Zermatt, Saas Fee and the Val d'Anniviers which are between 1 and 1.5 hours away.

## Town

As you sip a cold and expensive beer in the swanky town centre, you're left in no doubt that this is a premier Swiss resort. A huge golf course, streets lined entirely with Maseratis and numerous villas with helipads occupy this beautiful wooded plateau above Sierre in the heart of Switzerland. As you might imagine, the nightlife is a refined and dignified affair as opposed to a raucous night of debauchery, but there's a decent selection of bars and restaurants to choose from. Consider driving or taking the funicular down to Sierre and stocking up on supplies, as it presents a far less wallet-withering option if you're here for any length of time.

## Lift dates

The Plaine Morte cable car which gives you access to the big enduro lines mentioned above is open during July and August, but Cry d'Er and the park open from June to mid-October. The official dates and times can be found here: **tinyurl.com/crans-lifts**

You do have the option of dropping into the valley and catching the funicular back up from Sierre, but bear in mind that this does cost around 10 Euros a pop, so it can get expensive if you're here for any length of time. It runs pretty much year round so you can take advantage of it at any time during the season: **www.cie-smc.ch**

# Crans-Montana

## Maps

Both of the marked runs are well signed and easily found from the Cry d'Er lift so you won't be needing a map of the park. Using the Violettes and Plaine Morte cable cars requires a little more planning, but you'll find some great route ideas as well as detailed maps to download at Biking Spots: **www.bikingspots.ch**

The area crosses irritatingly over a number of maps, meaning you're probably best off downloading something from Biking Spots, as above. If you really want to spend your money, you're after the Swiss National Maps, numbers *1266*, *1267*, *1286* and *1287*.

## Where to stay

Camping Moubra is one of the best (and most affordable) options here. Situated near the main lake, this tranquil spot amongst the swaying pines of the plateau is a great place to chill after a day's riding and is close to the town centre: **www.campingmoubra.ch**

If you're only visiting for a couple of days then it's worth checking out the official site, which has long-weekend package deals on offer, including accommodation, food and lift passes: **tinyurl.com/crans-deals**

## Eating and drinking

For instant refreshment on the trails check out Bar 360, a popular spot situated next to the north shore zone at the bottom of the park that also serves light snacks during the day. If you head into town you'll notice this isn't the most wild venue on earth for a night out, but there are a couple of local hang-outs such as the Molino restaurant which is always busy due to the large and delicious pizzas that flow from the kitchen.

Late night 'chill bars' are the speciality here and you can do it in style at Leo's Bar and Taillens pub in Crans centre.

## Bike spares

Alex Sports is located next to the Cry d'Er lift, specialising in Kona hire bikes and those weird monster scooter things for anyone looking to experience instant death on the mountain. If you're in need of spares or mechanical support then head down to Bike Sport Erik in Sierre which has a good range of products in stock: **www.bikesporterick.ch**

◀ *The big one. Switchbacking towards the Lac de Tseuzier – Plaine Morte to Sion.*

# La Clusaz

La Clusaz remains well off the radar for most UK riders, but, with a great mix of wide open man-made blasts and technical forest singletrack, it really shouldn't be. If you're looking for an Alpine bike park experience without the crowds and knackered trails of the bigger resorts, look no further.

## Introduction

Access to La Clusaz is just as easy from Geneva as any of the northern Alps resorts, yet it receives very few visitors other than a handful of locals. That's a shame because a huge amount of work has gone into creating a bike park that's packed with high berms, north shore features and flat-out roller-coaster sections. Ok, it may not have the extensive area of the Portes du Soleil to play with, but you would be hard pressed to find anything there that's as long, well maintained or flowing as here in La Clusaz.

Even better is the natural stuff that lurks in the forest. Cut into the hillside, with big drops off to the side, are a number of winding singletracks that can be very technical, but still hugely satisfying to anyone who enjoys a rooty switchback or two.

## Trails

The riding focuses on two opposite mountain sides: the Crêt du Loup and the Beauregard, both of which can be accessed by lift from the town centre. It's a fifty/fifty choice, but my advice is to take a trip up to the Beauregard side first and follow the red run down through the forest to see a perfect example of what La Clusaz is all about. Flow is the name of the game here and enormous effort has been put into making sure that you never need to haul on the brakes or make sharp direction changes. The long sections of crests and dips, high bank turns and bridges over anything gnarly mean you can really get on the gas and launch the small jumps and drops along the way. There's also a whole lot of enduro to explore across the plateau and into the woods to the north of town too, so don't think that going straight down is the only option here.

It's a similar story on the Crêt du Loup side. The lift is a little higher, at 1,860 metres, so you do get some open trail above the tree line, but it's compacted earth rather than loose rock, so again you can sail through each section rather than fight your way down. From the mid station you're in the woods once again — probably the best part of the whole resort. Here you're presented with the enviable choice of hammering the swoopy man-made descent straight ahead, or taking on the adrenaline-filled singletracks to your right. Both present an orgy of drifting and carving through the forest loam, but it's the natural stuff with its sprawling root systems and rocky drops that provides the addictive 'terror and ecstasy all at the same time' sensation.

 INTERMEDIATE TO ADVANCED

 3

 80%

 20%

 3–4 DAYS

NOT TOO BAD

◀ Skirting the treeline, La Clusaz.

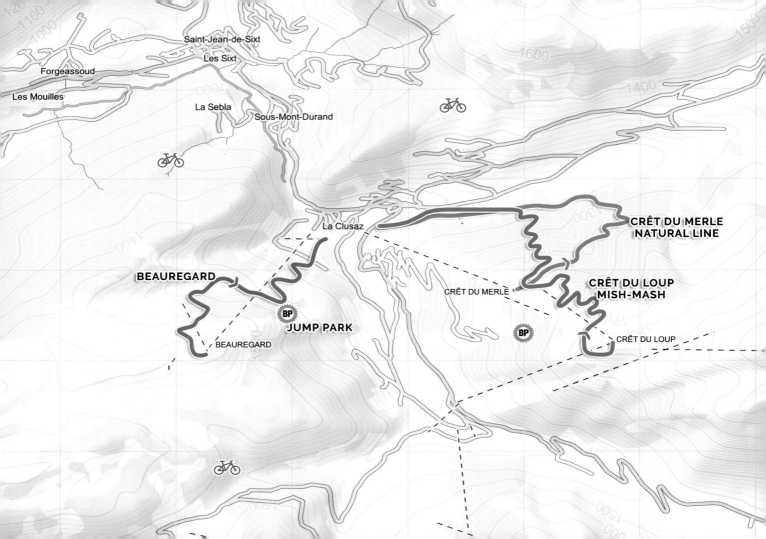

Forgeassoud

Les Mouilles

Saint-Jean-de-Sixt

Les Sixt

La Sebla

Sous-Mont-Durand

La Clusaz

**CRÊT DU MERLE
NATURAL LINE**

CRÊT DU MERLE

**CRÊT DU LOUP
MISH-MASH**

**BEAUREGARD**

**BP**

**JUMP PARK**

BEAUREGARD

**BP**

CRÊT DU LOUP

# La Clusaz

## Our pick

### CRÊT DU LOUP MISH-MASH

From the top lift take the marked descent straight ahead. Mini step-ups, crests and compressions make this an entertaining blast. Leave the main line at the mid station and head down the firetrack until you see a small trail dropping into the woods on your left. The huge grip generated by the loamy terrain allows you to hit drops, s-bends and natural jumps with speed and confidence. But beware, off-camber roots and tight switchbacks will soon wipe the smile off your face when they launch you into the deep gulley below.

### CRÊT DU MERLE NATURAL LINE

Head down the firetrack from the Crêt du Merle lift, ignoring the first singletrack option on the left (mentioned above). Continue on until you see a second, similar-looking trail on the left. This is much like the first option, except it pretty much takes a straight line cutting diagonally across the face. It goes without saying that this is extremely fast, which is a good thing because the best way to get over the rocky outcrops and twisted roots is to just carry the speed and launch them.

## Locals' choice

### JUMP PARK

Mid-way down the Beauregard trail you'll see a lake. Hang a left and pick up the north shore jump line in the trees. Here you'll find locals goading and mocking each other as they assess the sizeable drops whilst trying not to give in to peer pressure. The features actually all work well, which is more than can be said for the wobbly suspension bridge lower down – whatever you do don't ride on it two at a time.

## General info

The official website will leave you suitably confused and underwhelmed, as any good French MTB marketing should: **www.laclusaz.com**

Active Azur offer holidays in the area and give a good overview of the station: **www.activeazur.com**

## Getting here

La Clusaz sits in the Aravis mountain range between Chamonix and Lake Annecy. It's about an hour's drive from Geneva airport by car or by minibus transfer: **www.alp-line.com**

# La Clusaz

## Town

Few Alpine resorts are as picturesque as La Clusaz. Heidi-style chalets nestle beneath the jagged Aravis mountain range, making for proper chocolate-box scenes. It's a big town though and a popular ski destination for the French, so there's no shortage of accommodation available. Visitors from nearby Annecy and Geneva keep things busy throughout the summer season too, so you'll have no problem locating a beer and a burger, or hunting down some cow memorabilia in one of the many Alpine-themed gift shops. You're also not far from the stunning Lake Annecy if you fancy a chilled day off the bike.

## Lift dates

The lifts run permanently from the end of June to early September. Dates and times can be found here: tinyurl.com/clusaz-info

## Maps

You can get a trail map at either the Beauregard or Crêt du Merle lift stations. You can also see one online at **www.activeazur.com**

IGN map *3430 ET: La Clusaz/Grand-Bornand* just about covers the area, although you might also want *3531 OT: Megève* if you want to explore further south.

## Where to stay

There are many ski apartments to choose from in the summer. A quick search on **www.booking.com** will bring up most options.

Camping FranceLoc is just up the road with a swimming pool and apartments if you don't want to pitch a tent. Both I (Bike Alp) and Active Azur offer catered holidays in the area: **www.bike-alp.com** **www.activeazur.com**

## Eating and drinking

There are quite a few cafés and bars located around the main square near the Beauregard lift and you can find a bakery and supermarket on the main street. Le Bélier is a local favourite for crêpes and no-nonsense snacks, but if you need your Savoyard cheese fix then head to La Caléche. Les Caves du Paccaly is a chilled venue for an evening beer and if you're feeling up for it you can head to club L'Écluse or Club 18 on the weekends and hang with the youths.

## Bike spares

Sport Boutique has Scott hire bikes and a very basic selection of spares. The staff there can also put you in touch with local guides.

◄ The point at which everything changes – out of the meadows and into the trees.

LA CLUSAZ **69**

# La Grave

Wild, untamed and mostly forgotten as an MTB destination, La Grave is the polar opposite of nearby Les Deux Alpes. It may be a small area, but the technical singletracks, which have been given a helping hand along the way, would be on my list of the best kept secrets in the Alps.

## Introduction

Craning your neck upwards as you stand in the town, you'll see the gondola disappearing towards the mighty La Meije peaks and glaciers. It all looks pretty serious, and it is. There are no maps or grading systems here or *Attention! 50-Centimetre Drop!* warnings on the trails. It's all at your own risk and exactly the way Alpine riding should be.

La Grave made its name in the winter as a freeride zone. There are no marked pistes whatsoever, and the typical Courchevel poseur has probably never heard of it. The town prides itself on providing a real mountain experience for skiers and boarders, and the same goes for riders in the summer. The trails are rocky, rooty and totally natural in origin, with some tweaking by the locals in the form of gaps and drops. It's freeride in its rawest sense and, as a result, only a good level of rider will appreciate the place.

were built by apes ... a thousand years ago ... but the work that's been put in by the passionate locals works brilliantly, giving the technical trails a wonderful flow.

The only real downside is the small area to play with. With only one lift and just the immediate forest accessible, there's not a whole lot of exploring to be done. It's possible to do some XC loops on the Plateau d'Emparis on the other side of the valley for a day or two, but really you're only looking at a few days here before you're repeating everything (which would be fine by me).

The terrain here drains well, but beware that the trails in the thicker sections of forest lower down can be hellish in the wet, the peaty earth becoming a slippery paste. So it's best avoided directly after the rain.

## Trails

There's only one lift to be found in La Grave and bikers are only allowed up to the mid station at 2,400 metres. This allows for 1,000 metres of descent on each run though, so it's easily enough for some big descents. It's hugely popular with sightseers and hikers heading up to the glaciers and with no effort put into the trails or into publicity, you're unlikely to see any other bikes about the place. This is great news because the singletracks feel untouched, the challenges being roots, rocks and the occasional jump rather than braking bumps. Clearly there's been no official investment and some of the north shore sections look like they

## Our pick
### EVERYTHING

With no marked trails it's hard to suggest a single best route. Most stuff starts with a roll over some huge rock slabs out of the lift, the massive glaciers above adding a stunning backdrop. Below this there are trails everywhere, all of which end up at the river just below La Grave, which sits slightly up the hillside. You can't go too far wrong so navigation's not much of a problem. Just keep your eye out for new sections which are appearing all the time. Follow your nose and enjoy!

INTERMEDIATE TO ADVANCED

1

80%

20%

2–3 DAYS

NOT TOO BAD

◀ Roots, rocks and natural trails.  Photo: John Coefield

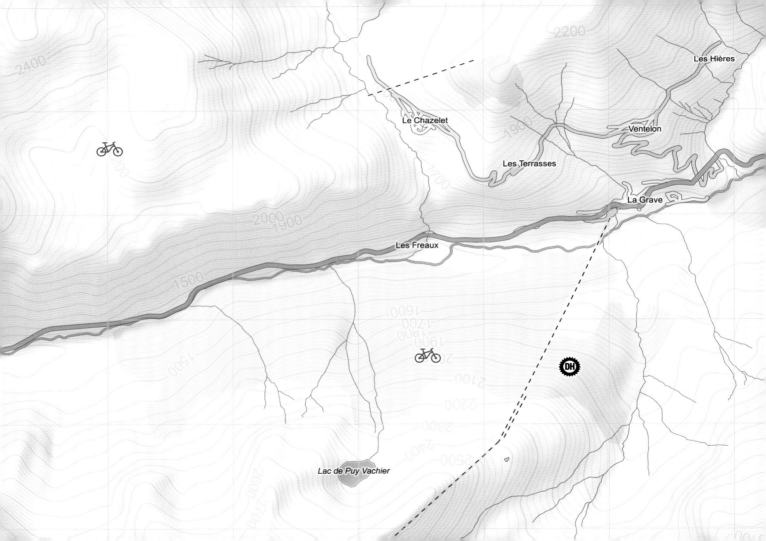

Les Hières

Le Chazelet

Ventelon

Les Terrasses

La Grave

Les Freaux

Lac de Puy Vachier

# La Grave

## General info

There's not a whole lot of info on La Grave in the summer and it's certainly not going to attract hordes of bikers any time soon. Basic info on opening times can be found at tinyurl.com/la-grave-info

## Getting here

The resort sits near the Col du Lautaret, about 30 minutes up the road from Les Deux Alpes and about 1 hour 45 minutes from Grenoble. Driving down or flying into Grenoble and then renting a hire car are the only real options.

## Town

La Grave is a small village sitting on the main road between Grenoble and Briançon. Les Deux Alpes isn't far to the west and Valloire and Serre Chevalier are within easy reach over the Galibier and Lautaret cols respectively. A lot of traffic passes through as a result and the bars and restaurants with views over the huge mountains above are busy during the day. The evening time is a different matter though, and you begin to realise why it's called 'the grave'. Everyone appears to be dead or missing, presumably in some extreme skiing accident, so it's not the place for great post-ride nightlife.

## Lift dates

Being a walking destination has its perks – the lift opens from mid-June to mid-September, longer than anywhere else in the area.

## Maps

Nothing really. You can get a 'map' at the lift which is a picture of a random hill with a yellow line on it. Better to get an IGN map in Bourg d'Oisans and keep a look out for the secret trails – *3436 ET: Meije/ Pelvoux* covers the main area.

## Where to stay

The Camping de la Meije is a lovely tranquil spot below the village and is in typical do-it-yourself La Grave style: **www.camping-delameije.com**

## Eating and drinking

There are a few bars and restaurants along the main street. Alp'Bar serves up snack style grub, while the Hôtel Castillan is a bit more upmarket and has stunning views over the glaciers above. Most of the bars are shut in the evenings so you won't be partying the night away.

## Bike spares

Not a lot to be found here. Your best bet is in Bourg d'Oisans. Au Cadre Rouge has a surprisingly useful set of spares inside and is only 20 to 30 minutes down the road.

# La Plagne

The most frustrating lift system in the world does a great job of keeping the masses away, leaving some brilliant high-mountain singletrack to the few that persevere. You'll be pedalling to reach the good stuff, but if solitary big days out on the mountain are high on your list, La Plagne is well worth checking out.

## Introduction

La Plagne has made an incredible effort to make its biking area unusable. Trying to tackle the random and disjointed lifts is a total headache that quickly sends the blood pressure soaring, while the ludicrous process of obtaining a lift pass will drive even the most balanced of minds to the verge of madness. By the time you finally make it on to the mountain, it's likely that you'll have an overwhelming urge to punch somebody. But try and focus, because despite all of this, La Plagne is home to some fantastic backcountry riding away from the crowds. Lonely singletracks pick their way along ridgelines and high plateaus before dropping into the forests below and, with no one else to ride them, they stay in superb condition. You could session descents in the many La Plagne villages dotted over the mountain, but really this area is all about big mountain adventure and making up your own itineraries.

## Trails

The mountainside contains the many La Plagne villages, all with their own mini bike parks and fantastic natural trails. Unfortunately the random lift opening times (that never seem to correspond with one another) make it virtually impossible to link them together. Therefore it would seem reasonable to base yourself at a central point such as La Roche, which is open more regularly. That's until you realise that it's not possible to buy a pass at the lift. That would be far too easy.

Instead, you need to head to the tourist info that's hidden deep within the sinister walls of 'Plagne Centre'. Clearly they don't get many requests for a mountain bike pass here, so don't be put off if the startled looks upon the staffs' faces implies that you just posed the question 'Excuse me, do you have any orphans for sale?' It's just something they've never heard before and the reason why the trails are so pristine. Even the main line from the top of the Roche de Mio back into Belle Plagne is as smooth as a millpond and great to blast down. However the sooner you leave the park the better, because the forgotten singletracks that drop into the valleys are sensational. These offer very long descents, particularly into the Champagny valley, but expect a bit of a slog to get back over the ridge. The terrain is varied too, from exposed rocky singletrack up top to the swoopy forest loam around Plan Gagnant.

Those looking to smash around a bike park won't get a lot out of this area, but if you're willing to use a map, do a little exploring and battle with the lift system, the rewards are huge.

INTERMEDIATE TO ADVANCED

8

50%

50%

3–4 DAYS

TRICKY

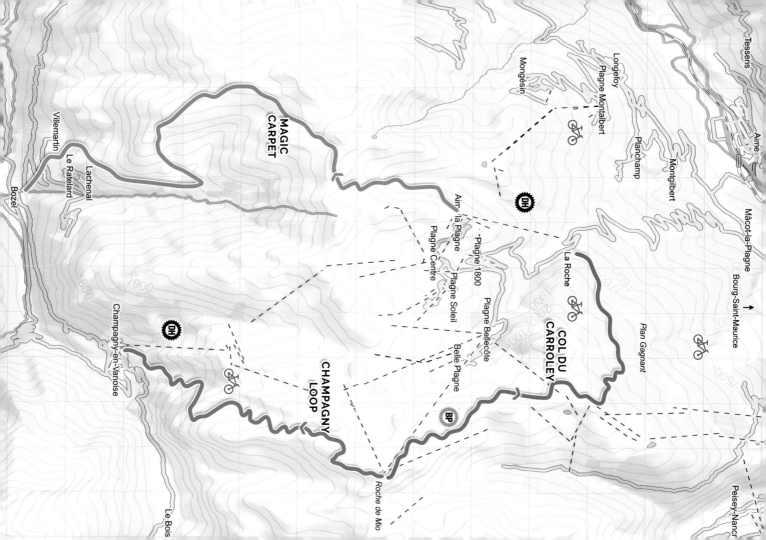

# La Plagne

## Our pick

### COL DU CARROLEY

From the top of the Roche de Mio lift, drop straight into the marked red descent back towards Belle Plagne. After passing through the tunnel, take a right and climb up to the Col du Carroley. Ignore the marked routes and take the singletrack to the left. Cutting right and heading back on yourself, you'll soon be riding a sublime and exposed trail overlooking the valley. Drop left into the woods for a fast and swoopy feast all the way back to La Roche.

### CHAMPAGNY LOOP

Again, start from from the Roche de Mio lift, but this time head straight along the top of the ridge before making your own line back to the firetrack on your right. Take a left passing behind the Roc du Sérac. Heading through the rocky landscape, you'll soon pick up a very flowing trail that takes in magnificent views over the Champagny valley, before dropping through the woods on endless switchbacks. Enjoy it because after you take the lift from Champagny, there's a big climb back over the ridge into La Plagne.

## Locals' choice

### MAGIC CARPET

Sam and the boys at Bike Village are pretty keen on the *Magic Carpet* run off the Roche chairlift. A 25-kilometre descent drops you into the untouched woodlands of La Plagne and down to the valley below. Unfortunately, getting back can be a logistical nightmare so some insider knowledge is the key here. Give Sam a shout at **www.bikevillage.co.uk**

## General info

There's not a whole lot of information out there to be honest. The official site (**tinyurl.com/la-plagne-biking**) has some basic info, but you're better off contacting the local companies who offer guided trips in the area. Bike Village have a wealth of knowledge on the area: **www.bikevillage.co.uk**

## Getting here

La Plagne sits high up the mountainside above Aime, just across the valley from Bourg-Saint-Maurice and Les Arcs. Grenoble is around 150 kilometres, and Geneva about 200 kilometres away. The train runs to Aime or Bourg-Saint-Maurice so that's another option, but you'll need transport when you're there. **www.voyages-sncf.com**

# La Plagne

## Town

Arriving at the foot of the mountain, it's clear that this isn't going to be easy. A road sign lists hundreds of La Plagne variants, all of which are totally dead during the summer. Each village has its own lift, which may or may not be running on a given day, so you'll need a car or uplifts to get around as well. For these reasons it's best to stay in nearby Bourg-Saint-Maurice which has many accommodation options as well as bars and restaurants. From there you can organise some day trips to the La Plagne area by car or via the Vanoise Express lift from Les Arcs.

## Lift dates

The lifts open during July and August. However, many don't open on weekends, only certain ones open on Mondays (but not every week), different ones on Wednesdays and Thursdays, and it's anyone's guess on Fridays. You can attempt to work it out at: **tinyurl.com/la-plagne-lift**

## Maps

The tourist info might have a map kicking around, but a safer bet is to download one from the lift web page: **tinyurl.com/la-plagne-lift** Otherwise, IGN *3532 ET: Les Arcs/La Plagne* and *3532 OT: Massif du Beaufortain* cover the riding here.

## Where to stay

Staying in Bourg-Saint-Maurice or Les Arcs and then accessing La Plagne by car or the Vanoise Express is the best idea. You could do worse than the Chill Chalet (**www.chillchalet.com**) or the Loft (**www.loftbourg.com**) in Bourg. There's also a good campsite at nearby Landry: **www.camping-eden-savoie.com**, as well Bike Village who offer accommodation and guiding in the area: **www.bikevillage.co.uk**

## Eating and drinking

For a welcome break from the Savoyard cheese fest, head to Globetrotter in Bourg, which offers tasty international food at a good price. If you really can't resist, the refuge and brasserie in the centre will supply the cheese.

Bazoom and the Tonneau bar near the funicular are two bars worth checking out for a good post-ride atmosphere.

## Bike spares

The Intersport in Bourg-Saint-Maurice is really quite good and stocks one of the biggest selections of spares you'll find in the Alps. Revolver bike shop nearby doesn't have so much in the way of spares but is great for mechanical assistance. Startline MTB is based in Tignes but will deliver Specialized hire bikes to your door in Bourg-Saint-Maurice or La Plagne: **startlinemtb.com**

# La Rosière

La Rosière may not be the biggest standalone area, but the wooded hillsides hide a multitude of top-quality natural trails that make it well worth a visit from nearby Les Arcs.

## Introduction

La Rosière sits high on the sunny slopes above Bourg-Saint-Maurice. It's a popular spot for bike chalets based in Les Arcs as well as those offering multi-destination tours through the Alps, and it's easy to see why. Superb trails snake off into the valley below, offering stunning backdrops and the ultimate in Alpine singletrack photo opportunities. It's also ideally positioned if you're driving between spots, lying directly en route to Les Arcs and Tignes from La Thuile, Pila or Chamonix. Clearly the main draws here are the flowing forest trails rather than the marked runs at the top of the mountain, but mixing them up makes for some varied and long descents that anyone apart from the complete beginner will have a blast on. The low rider numbers ensure that the trails stay nice and smooth too, so you don't need a downhill-specific machine to enjoy them.

## Trails

The two chairlifts that run during the summer really define the different terrain styles on offer. From the main La Rosière village, the Roches Noires Express takes you to up to a rocky and barren world and the starting point for the majority of the marked descents. They're shaley, fast and proper all-weather trails that are fun to ride, but they don't exactly leave you gagging for more. A better bet is to leave the DH bike behind and pedal up from the lift to the Col de la Traversette, where you can exploit a number of fantastic natural trails that swing out wide into the valley. This really begins to open up an otherwise limited riding area.

The Ecudets chairlift serves the woodlands below the village and it's here that you'll find the properly good stuff. You won't see any of the natural lines on the trail map, but climb up the road a little and you're presented with irresistible-looking singletracks that switchback endlessly through the forests below. Even in here the forest floor remains stony and flinty in nature, so they'll never get slimy in the wet. That said, they'll never be as amazing in the dry as the deep forest loam that can be found further north ...

In the winter the resort is linked with La Thuile in Italy. This link isn't possible using the lifts alone in the summer, but an hour of climbing and traversing from the Roches Noires lift will get you there. The trails in La Thuile are some of the best that the Alps has to offer, so if you're willing to put in some leg work you can open up a superb riding area that's well off the UK biking radar.

| | |
|---|---|
|  | INTERMEDIATE TO ADVANCED |
| | 2 |
| | 70% |
| | 30% |
| | 2–3 DAYS |
| | NOT TOO BAD |

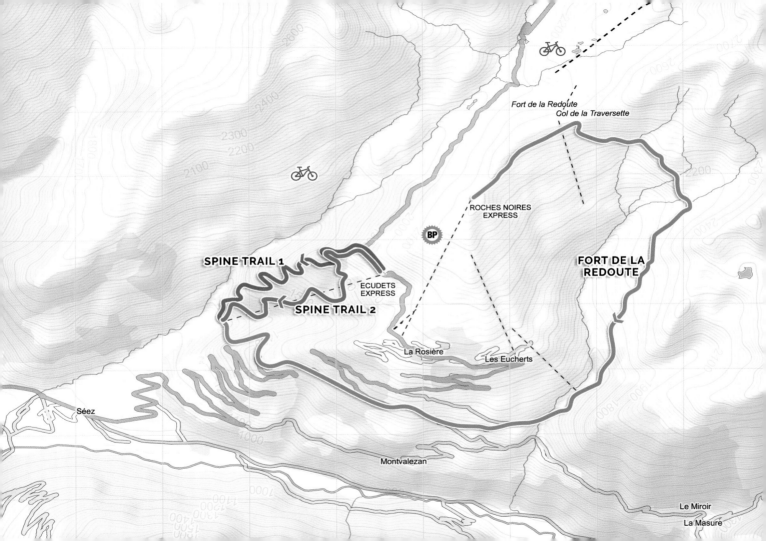

# La Rosière

## Our pick
### SPINE TRAIL 1
From the top of the Ecudets lift, climb up the road for 5 minutes. You'll easily spot the mouth-watering singletrack clinging to the spine on your left. As the trail heads left off the ridgeline keep your eye out for a small and unmarked path on your right. This will take you on a joyous switchback journey through the forest all the way to the lift station.

### FORT DE LA REDOUTE
Head straight out the back of the Roches Noires chairlift and climb up the ridgeline to the Fort de la Redoute. Head down the large firetrack to the right before picking up a singletrack that contours through the moorland terrain. The trail traverses on to the other side of the valley and then drops at warp speed through the lower meadows and forests, bringing you out at Le Chatelard. Cut right back across the hillside through Les Laix and Planardin to hook up with the Ecudets lift.

## Locals' choice
### SPINE TRAIL 2
Taking the same ridgeline singletrack as *Spine Trail 1*, simply follow the trail round to the left and pick up the marked run back to the lift. With a few berms added to the mix, this makes for a great mash-up of the natural and man-made features that make La Rosière so good.

## General info
You can find extremely basic info on the official site: **summer.larosiere.net**

A better bet is to contact the numerous local companies that operate in the area: **www.whiteroomchalet.com**, **www.bikevillage.co.uk**, **www.trailaddiction.com**

## Getting here
La Rosière can be found on the Col du Petit Saint-Bernard above Bourg-Saint-Maurice, around 2 hours from Grenoble airport by car. It's also easily accessed from the Italian side via the Mont Blanc tunnel, 1.5 hours' drive from Chamonix. You're best staying in Bourg-Saint-Maurice which can be reached by train or minibus transfer: **www.thecoolbus.co.uk** and **www.voyages-sncf.com**

## Town
La Rosière is a great spot for a post-ride sunset beer, as it offers beautiful views over the surrounding peaks and valleys. It makes for a pleasant overnight stop, but if you're planning on staying for a longer period, it's better to head for nearby Bourg-Saint-Maurice where you can find many more accommodation options, bars, restaurants and bike shops. You're also much better positioned here for day trips to the many great biking destinations in the area, including Les Arcs, La Plagne and the Trois Vallées.

# La Rosière

## Lift dates
The two chairlifts run from early July to the end of August. Specific times and dates can be found at **tinyurl.com/larosiere-lifts**

## Maps
A trail map is available at the Roches Noires chairlift in La Rosière. Detailed maps are tricky – IGN *3532 ET: Les Arcs/La Plagne* covers the immediate area, but riding over to La Thuile will require Italian IGC map 107: *Monte Bianco/Courmayer/La Thuile.*

## Where to stay
Bourg-Saint-Maurice is the better place to stay. There's easy access to the Ecudets lift either by a short drive or by taking the bus to Séez and then a short pedal. Good accommodation options are the Chill Chalet (**www.chillchalet.com**) and the Loft (**www.loftbourg.com**).

Also check out the campsite: **www.camping-bourgsaintmaurice.com**

## Eating and drinking
If Savoyard cuisine isn't your thing then head to Globetrotter in Bourg which offers tasty international food at a good price. If you can't resist the local cheese fest then the refuge and brasserie in the centre will oblige in blocking your arteries.

Bazoom and the Tonneau bar near the funicular are two bars worth checking out for a good post ride atmosphere.

## Bike spares
The Intersport in Bourg-Saint-Maurice is really quite good and stocks one of the biggest selections of spares you'll find in the Alps. Revolver bike shop nearby doesn't have so much in the way of spares but is great for mechanical assistance. Startline MTB is based in Tignes but will deliver Specialized hire bikes to your door in Bourg-Saint-Maurice or La Rosière: **startlinemtb.com**

◄ La Rosière bike park.

# La Thuile

It's very rare that man can rival Mother Nature in trail design, but the demi-gods at La Thuile have done just that. This understated Italian bike park delivers some of the best man-made singletrack on earth. If quality rather than quantity is your thing, then look no further.

## Introduction

La Thuile lies at the foot of the Col du Petit Saint-Bernard, within spitting distance of Les Arcs and La Rosière – although drooling or salivating would be more appropriate in this case, as the glorious singletrack here beats anything on the French side of the mountain.

Much like Pila or Sauze, these trails have the signature Italian fun factor written all over them – there are jumps, drops and technical sections, but all of it leaves you whooping with ecstasy rather than howling in terror ... Try thinking of the best natural trail you know in the UK, then add some subtle berms, kickers and hips, quadruple it in length and then imagine there's been a drought for four years. You now have some idea as to what awaits you in La Thuile.

## Trails

With only two chairlifts and one mountainside to play with, the trail network at La Thuile doesn't look massively exciting, but don't be put off. While some bike parks feel the need to cover a hillside with twenty versions of exactly the same mediocre run, the local chaps here have put a lot of time and effort into creating just a few brilliant ones.

The grin factor is instantaneous straight out of the lift, as the gentle terrain above the tree line allows you to get off the brakes and really charge. Weaving through the shrubs and rocky outcrops, you'll soon find yourself in wild surroundings, with glaciers, majestic ridges and mountain streams lending a proper backcountry sensation to it all.

Things get even better in the woods lower down, where the already-brilliant natural singletrack has been delicately shaped to carry maximum speed. This is especially true when you drop to the Pont Serrand, where every feature has been remodelled to get you airborne, flat out and sideways – but without losing any of that all-important natural feel. The dry and sandy terrain lends itself well to this type of riding, encouraging constant rear wheel lock ups without the risk of serious trail degradation.

About the only downside is the limited area of the park. For that reason it's best to forget the DH machine and come armed with a trail bike. That way you can climb over the col and drop into La Rosière (page 81) on the other side of the mountain. This immediately doubles your riding area and is still covered on the same lift pass. Remember to save some energy for the way back though, as the Rosière lifts don't get you high enough to simply roll back into La Thuile.

(page 81)

 **ENDURO**

 INTERMEDIATE TO ADVANCED

 2

 90%

 10%

 3–4 DAYS

NOT TOO BAD

◄ A bike park like no other – *Maisonettes* trail.

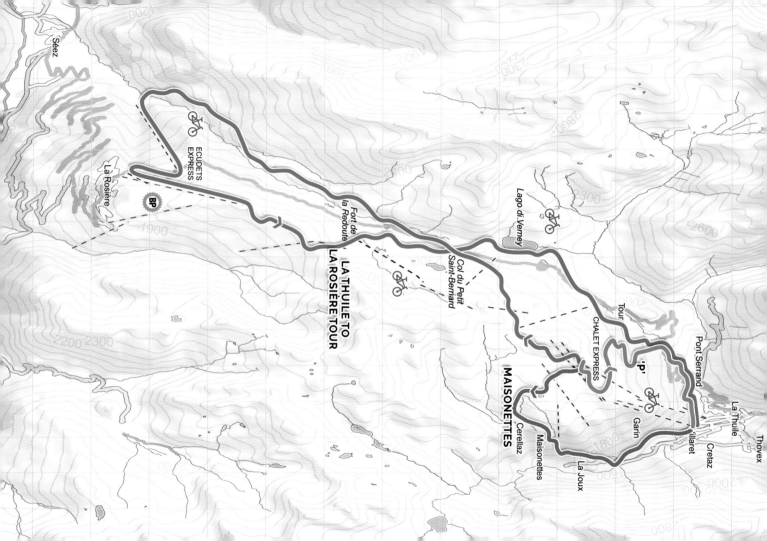

Séez

ECUDETS
EXPRESS

La Rosière

BP

1900

Fort de
la Redoute

Col du Petit
Saint-Bernard

LA THUILE TO
LA ROSIÈRE TOUR

2200 2300

Lago di Verney

CHALET
EXPRESS

Tour

MAISONETTES

'P'

Pont Serrand

La Thuile

Thovex

Garin

Cerellaz

Maisonettes

La Joux

Filaret

Cretaz

1800

# La Thuile

## Our pick
### MAISONETTES

For a proper 'out there' feel, head for the runs marked *K* and *K2* from the Chalet Express lift. The snaking stony path leads you into ever more stunning territory at every turn. Some technical sections next to the river give way to the fast-rolling forest floor, deep in pine needles. With a perfect gradient and the odd root to pop off, you can really get on the gas here. From La Joux, follow a path that criss-crosses the road back to the valley floor.

### LA THUILE TO LA ROSIÈRE TOUR

You'll need to climb out of the top lift to the small col above you, following the marked *Comino* path. Drop down to the lake and the Col du Petit Saint-Bernard. From here you can pick up the GR5 walking trail and charge through the meadows to Saint-Germain before taking the road down to the Ecudets lift. Sample a few descents in La Rosière before making your way back to the Fort de la Redoute and then head to Lake Verney and pick up the marked *T* route into Pont Serrand, linking up with the black trail into La Thuile.

## Locals' choice
### 'P'

Trail centre meets Mother Nature's finest; the route simply marked as '*P*' is a stonker. This fast and flowing line will take you on a roller coaster ride all the way to Pont Serrand, where you can climb the road a little to pick up the black *Garin* trail into the town.

## General info

The official tourism website has plenty of info on the park, lifts and the town itself: **www.lathuile.it**

Many companies in nearby Les Arcs offer tours here: **www.whiteroomchalet.com**, **www.bikevillage.co.uk**, **www.trailaddiction.com**

## Getting here

La Thuile is around 2 hours from Geneva by car, via Chamonix and the Mont Blanc Tunnel. It's also easily reached from Bourg-Saint-Maurice and Les Arcs over the Col du Petit Saint-Bernard. Turin airport is also an option at just over 2 hours away by car. Transfers from Grenoble, Geneva or the train station at Bourg-Saint-Maurice can be arranged through Coolbus: **www.thecoolbus.co.uk** and **www.voyages-sncf.com**

# La Thuile

## Town

La Thuile is an idyllic mountain town, where slate houses in the traditional Italian style huddle beneath the giant peaks. It's bigger than first appearances suggest, with a surprisingly vibrant centre. It's not exactly rowdy, but a good selection of fancy bars and ice cream parlours should keep a happy biker even happier after the lifts close. Being part of the San Bernardo ski system, it's easy to find empty and reasonably priced accommodation during the summer season as well.

## Lift dates

The lifts are generally open from July through to early September. Give the tourist office a shout for specific dates: **info@lathuile.net**

## Maps

A trail map is available at the Bosco Express chairlift. Italian IGC map 107: *Monte Bianco/Courmayeur/La Thuile* also covers the area, and you might want the French IGN *3532 ET: Les Arcs/La Plagne* if you're riding over to La Rosière.

## Where to stay

There's no shortage of ski accommodation here, with many hotels and apartments offering good deals in the summer. The tourism info site has a good selection to choose from: **www.lathuile.net**. Also check out Hotel Planibel right opposite the main lift: **tinyurl.com/Planibel-Hotel**

Bike-specific chalets in the Les Arcs area often offer day trips here as part of a package: **www.whiteroomchalet.com**, **www.bikevillage.co.uk**, **www.trailaddiction.com**

## Eating and drinking

A relaxed vibe makes post-ride chilling a very pleasant activity here. The Pepita Café is a must for delicious freshly prepared dishes and limoncello in chocolate shot glasses! Look for the totem pole above the town square. The self-proclaimed 'biker friendly' Brasserie de Bathieu is a no-frills relaxed spot in the centre where you can hang out, drink a Peroni and play backgammon with the locals.

Nip across to the crèmerie at the bottom of the Bosco lift for a tasty mid-ride cake.

## Bike spares

The chaps at Only Ski feel the name lends itself well to the rental of mountain bikes. Near the Bosco lift, they have a random selection of rental bikes, basic spares and a bike wash area.

# Les Arcs

The bike park at Les Arcs may not be the best the Alps has to offer, but the large network of unmarked singletrack lurking in the woods is properly good. The best stuff is hard to find though, so try to ride with someone in the know or you may be a little underwhelmed.

## Introduction

The trail map looks impressive enough, with a range of green to black runs catering for most abilities. It's mostly run of the mill stuff though and because the majority of the park is above the tree line there's little to distinguish one bermed trail from the next. There are big descents to be had with almost 2,000 metres of height loss, so it's not terrible, but there are better options if park is your thing.

The real draw to this place is the sweet singletrack hidden in the woods, none of which can be found on the map. Rooty, rocky and great fun for experienced riders, you'll either need to hire a guide or spend a week creeping around the woods looking for a trailhead. If you have transport or join a guided trip you can explore the wider area of La Plagne and La Rosière as well.

## Trails

Any resort that ranges from high mountain passes down to the valley-floor forest is going to offer a great variety of riding and Les Arcs is no exception. The lift system gives you access to trails from 750 to 2,500 metres, meaning big descents that can cover high-up rocky blasts and tight rooty switchbacks in a single run. The fast-draining shale up top also gives some good all-weather riding if the woodlands get a little hairy. The area is well positioned for exploring further afield too. La Plagne's trails can be accessed via the Vanoise Express and La Rosière is within reach as well if you have some transport, so there's plenty here to keep you occupied for a week or longer. But to do that you will need some insider knowledge, as the best stuff really is very tricky to find.

Sam who runs Bike Village sums up the area well: 'If you want to get the most from the Les Arcs area, leave the DH bike at home and grab the enduro/trail rig – the marked resort trails will not keep you busy for long but the singletrack that can be accessed from the local lifts could keep you going for months. It has a very natural feel and bike traffic is minimal so a truly "out there" experience is very attainable. There are trails to suit less experienced riders but overall the steepness of the valley sides and the tight switchbacks mean that experienced riders will have more fun. As nothing is marked out, if you want to ride trails that will push you but leave you grinning, whatever your ability, it really is crucial to have a guide who knows the area inside out.'

If you'd rather go it alone then you should look both above and below the main system for the good bits. The *Sketchy Dismount* route described overleaf is a high-mountain epic that's well worth the short climb to the Lac des Moutons from the top of the Transarc lift. Perhaps even better though are the cheeky trails to be found in the woodlands above Landry and also in the steep Malgovert forest which can be accessed from the road linking Arc 1600 and 1950. Expect many roots, tight switchbacks and a huge grin by the time you reach the valley floor.

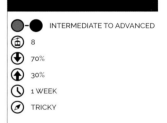

| | INTERMEDIATE TO ADVANCED |
| --- | --- |
| 8 | |
| 70% | |
| 30% | |
| 1 WEEK | |
| TRICKY | |

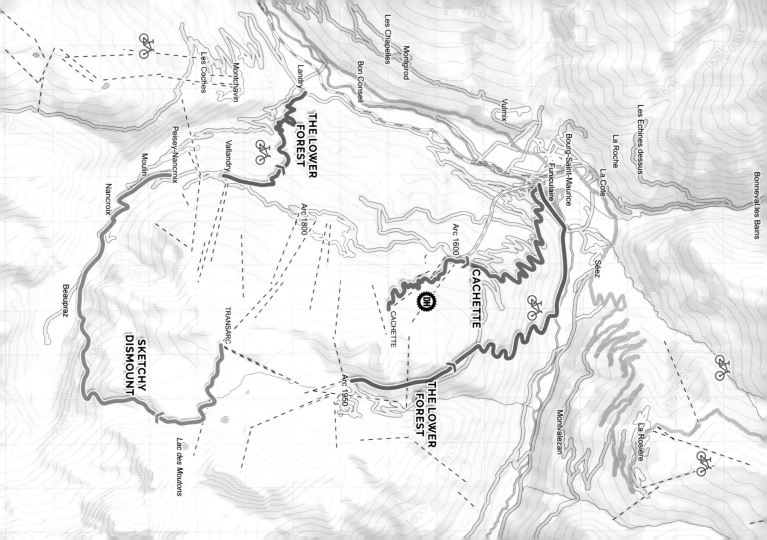

# Les Arcs

## Our pick
### SKETCHY DISMOUNT
One of the classic big-mountain routes, this stunning trail off the Lac des Moutons offers everything from fast-rolling hardpack to very technical and exposed sections – as evidenced in the title. If you make it past the loopy hounds of hell that guard the sheep up top, you can enjoy a huge singletrack descent dropping 1,200 metres, all the way down to the village of Beaupraz. Head down into Peisey and take the Lonzagne lift back into the system.

### THE LOWER FORESTS
The steep woodlands below the Les Arcs resorts are littered with fantastic singletracks. Technical rooted sections and rocky drops require a lot of concentration, but get a line hooked up and they flow incredibly well. Particularly good are the secret lines from Arc 1950 and in the forest between Vallandry and Landry. They may not be easy to spot, but trust me, they're in there.

## Locals' choice
### CACHETTE
For the local companies it's all about exploring the off-piste singletrack, but the park isn't all bad and local DH boys will session the *Cachette* black run all day long. Unlike the rest of the park, the trail has plenty of features including big jumps and high speed rocky sections. It is proper good fun on a big DH rig and can be ridden all the way into Bourg-Saint-Maurice for a great 'end of the day' blast.

## General info
Les Arcs is a pretty efficient setup when it comes to biking, with lots of info out there on the lifts, trails and bike-specific chalets on offer. The Les Arcs site gives a clear and concise overview of the park: **www.lesarcsnet.com/biking**

Local companies have been riding here a long time and have spent years building up knowledge of the area. Bike Village and trailAddiction both operate locally: **www.bikevillage.co.uk** and **www.trailaddiction.com**.

## Getting here
Bourg-Saint-Maurice is most easily accessed via Albertville and Moûtiers, around 1 hour 15 minutes by car from Chambéry. Grenoble, Chambéry and Geneva are options for flights. Contact Cool Bus for transfers: **www.thecoolbus.co.uk**

The train is also an option from Paris or Geneva to Bourg-Saint-Maurice: **www.voyages-sncf.com**

# Les Arcs

## Town

There may be some decent views up here, but the Les Arcs resorts are about as charming as downtown Detroit. A far better option is to stay in Bourg-Saint-Maurice at the foot of the mountain, which has a vibrant old town and plenty of bars and restaurants to choose from. It's only a 10-minute ride up the funicular to access the trails and a much more central base from which to explore the nearby resorts.

## Lift dates

The lifts open during July and August. Specific dates and prices can be found at tinyurl.com/lesarcs-lifts

## Maps

A map can be obtained from the tourist office at Bourg-Saint-Maurice or at any of the Les Arcs resorts. You can also find one online here: tinyurl.com/lesarcs-maps

IGN map *3532 ET: Les Arcs/La Plagne* covers the area at 1:25,000.

## Where to stay

Bourg-Saint-Maurice has plenty of accommodation on offer. The Chill Chalet (**www.chillchalet.com**) and the Loft (**www.loftbourg.com**) are both good options. Also check out the campsite: **www.camping-bourgsaintmaurice.com**

Bike Village and trailAddiction can offer accommodation, guiding and airport transfer packages. See their websites above.

## Eating and drinking

If Savoyard cuisine isn't your thing head to Globetrotter in Bourg, which offers tasty international food at a good price. If you can't resist the local cheese fest then the refuge and brasserie in the centre will oblige in blocking your arteries.

Bazoom and the Tonneau bar near the funicular are two bars worth checking out for a good post-ride atmosphere.

## Bike spares

The Intersport in Bourg-Saint-Maurice is really quite good and stocks one of the biggest selections of spares you'll find in the Alps. Revolver bike shop nearby doesn't have so much in the way of spares but is great for mechanical assistance. Startline MTB is based in Tignes but will deliver specialized hire bikes to your door in Bourg-Saint-Maurice or Les Arcs: **startlinemtb.com**

◄ 'A truly "out there" experience is very attainable.'

# Les Deux Alpes

With a huge number of man-made descents and many summer events including Crankworx Europe, Les Deux Alpes is pushing itself as the Alps' biggest and best bike park.

## Introduction

Les Deux Alpes' relentless pursuit of becoming the No. 1 destination in the Alps has certainly placed it on the international stage. The Mountain of Hell enduro race is a shameless copy of the Megavalanche across the valley in Alpe d'Huez, while the hosting of Crankworx clearly promotes the area as a freeride venue. It's not a huge riding area, but the mountainside is littered with trails for all abilities, some of them very long indeed. Make no mistake though, this is bike park through and through, with endless incarnations of berms, tabletops and doubles to keep the park-addict happy. The artificial nature of the trails means absolutely anyone could ride here. Even if you've never seen a bike before you'll be able to cruise the green and blue runs, and with no real option for backcountry stuff, even blind riders should be able to navigate their way around.

## Trails

Although very close to Alpe d'Huez, Les Deux Alpes is more in competition with the likes of the Portes du Soleil. Both areas are laced with no-nonsense descents full of berms, jumps and teeth-shattering braking bumps. I actually got tennis elbow on a blue run here. Despite its claims of being the 'biggest', the area falls a long way short of Morzine or Les Gets (for example), which are part of a huge network of trails. It's also possible to ride anywhere you like up there, but here in Les Deux Alpes you are restricted to the marked bike runs (it's forbidden to ride on the walking paths) so you're actually quite limited.

However, what you don't find in places like Les Gets are the huge descents that you get in Deux Alpes, such as the run from the glacier down to Venosc, dropping over 2,000 metres. With such lofty heights you also get that big mountain feel even though you're within a controlled environment.

The routes are all clearly marked and graded so you can really just switch off, ride your bike and have fun without the concentration required on the natural stuff. Adrenaline can still be had of course, with some big jumps and drops built into the black runs and in the 'playful zone' at the bottom of the Jandri lift. If you're looking for very long, trail centre style descents, then you won't find anything better in the area.

BEGINNER TO ADVANCED

8

90%

10%

1 WEEK

REALLY EASY

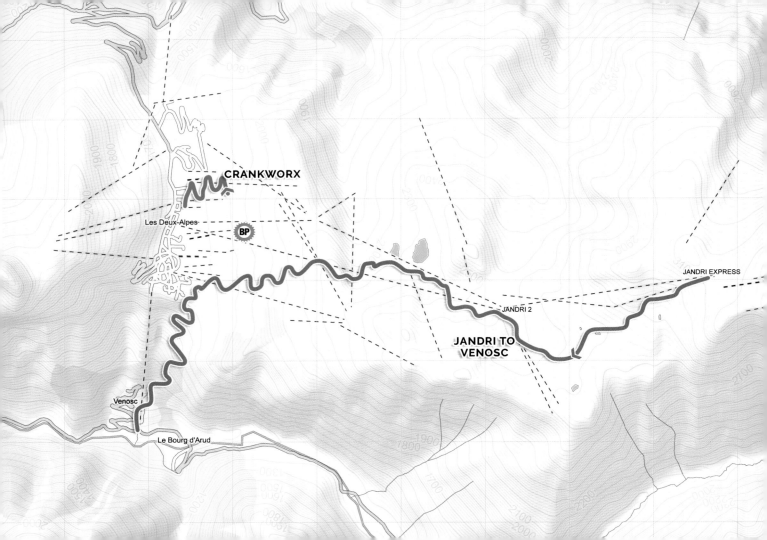

CRANKWORX

Les Deux-Alpes

BP

Venosc

Le Bourg d'Arud

JANDRI EXPRESS

JANDRI 2

JANDRI TO
VENOSC

# Les Deux Alpes

## Our pick
### JANDRI TO VENOSC
Riding from 3,200 metres is always going to be special. Super fast on fairly mellow and shaley terrain, it feels like you're blasting across the face of Mars. Cutting across to the *Diable* or *666* run into the resort, you can then hook up with the run into Venosc. This is possibly one of the most fun descents here, with plenty of step-ups and fast, heavily bermed sections.

## Locals' choice
### CRANKWORX
Ok, this is watching rather than riding, but it's simply awesome to witness. This and the Châtel Slopestyle are the only places in the Alps that you're likely to see all the big names going at it. So if you're in the area at the time (usually second week of July) you have to go and see these guys launch themselves over the huge gaps. Backflips become so ordinary after a few runs that you're likely to give one a go yourself afterwards, believing it to be easier than simply riding along the ground. Don't.

## General info
Les Deux Alpes has a dedicated bike park site which has everything you need to know about the trails and events throughout the summer: **www.2alpes-bikepark.com**

For more ideas on routes in the wider area, pick up the free *VTT EN OISANS* guidebook from the Venosc tourist info. It's pretty good and covers just about everything in the area.

## Getting here
The resort sits on the opposite side of the valley to Alpe d'Huez. Just continue through Bourg and after 20 minutes or so you'll see the signs on the right. If you're not driving down then flying into Grenoble or Chambéry and renting a hire car is your best bet. It's about 1.5 hours from Grenoble.

# Les Deux Alpes

## Town

As with Alpe d'Huez, the resort doesn't do pretty or picturesque – it's a full-on seasonal resort. But with the huge push in mountain biking, it's far from dead in the evenings. In fact it's one the liveliest summer resorts you're likely to stay in, particularly during the event weeks. English seems to be the common language here too, so it's very easy to hang out and chat with the locals. It's not a huge town but definitely big enough to keep you occupied for a week.

## Lift dates

Normally the end of June to the end of August but this will probably vary from year to year so always check: tinyurl.com/deuxalpes-lifts

## Maps

Bike maps are available from the tourist info in the town centre and at the ticket office at the lifts (Deux Alpes and Venosc). As the riding here is all about the park, you can find the trails without an IGN map – but if you want one, it's *3336 ET: Les Deux Alpes*.

## Where to stay

There's a large number of apartments and hotels to choose from. The resort website's *hébergement* page is really good, with many apartments and package deals on accommodation and lift passes: www.2alpes-vacances.com

## Eating and drinking

There's plenty going on here during the peak weeks and many of the winter bars and restaurants stay open during the summer. Smithy's Tavern is well worth a visit, with a great atmosphere in the bar and properly good, simple grub.

The Polar Bear Pub is a friendly spot in the centre of town. With good ales and an outside log burner on the terrace, it's a nice spot to chill. If you've got the energy then you can hang with the kids at the Avalanche Club until the wee hours.

## Bike spares

There are quite a few ski/bike shops in the resort offering a reasonable selection of spares. Camp d'Base has Kona hire bikes and a fair bit of kit for sale. Brun Sports also has a large stock of Trek hire bikes and a decent amount of spares. There are many others on the main streets.

◄ Wide trails mean high speeds. Deux Alpes.

# Les Saisies

The little-known resort of Les Saisies may not be as high or as extensive as other destinations, but the bike park they've created is a true lesson in how to build fun and sustainable trails. From rolling green runs to huge jumps and lengthy enduro routes, all levels are catered for.

## Introduction

With less than 300 vertical metres to play with, the high plateau of Les Saisies doesn't seem like an obvious choice for Alpine exploits. However, trails that make clever use of the terrain and keep their height with flowing turns rather than vertical lines make this one of the most enjoyable bike parks in the central Alps. Long, smooth and swoopy creations mean you couldn't wish for a better place for a beginner, while big jumps, gaps and north shore features provide more air time on the black run alone than many other parks put together.

There's room for adventure too if you're happy to explore, with huge enduro-style descents of up to eighteen kilometres in length into the valleys below and a bus service to bring you back up, as well as the possibility of linking into the Megève system to the north.

## Trails

French towns often display something typical or famous of the region as you enter them – a giant cheese or champagne bottle, or maybe a large turnip motif emblazoned upon the town sign. Not Les Saisies. Here you'll be greeted by a mountain biker statue with impressive levels of detail, such as disc brakes, 650b wheels and a classic four-bar linkage system. Clearly these guys are into mountain biking and if you're anything like me that will get you properly excited. You should be too because the fanaticism is even more evident up on the trails.

While many parks have lines that scrub too much speed, degrade quickly or are just plain boring, you get the feeling that everything here has been designed by a proper enthusiast with the aim of creating a park that can remain fun even after a season of heavy use. The mellow gradients do make this job easier as you can pretty well forget about the brakes, especially on the beginner trails, but even they have enough going on to keep things interesting. This same sense of flow is evident right through to the black run, where simply rolling through the long and sweeping turns is enough to clear the big gaps and wooden features.

Then there's the enduro. The plateau may seem limited, but with regular(ish) buses running back up from the valleys below, it's possible to ride some epic singletrack through the lower woodlands into Beaufort and Albertville. Try heading off Mont Bisanne, opposite the lift system, for starters (see 'Our pick'). Using public transport may seem a bit of a fuss at first, but that's kind of a good thing because it means that no one rides these loamy forest lines and they remain in superb condition. The best routes from the station are marked too, so they're fairly easy to follow without a whole lot of planning.

If all this isn't enough then a climb up the ridgeline to the Col de Basse-Combe will let you descend into Megève and access the lifts there, creating a huge riding area if you've got the energy.

| | |
|---|---|
| ●–● | BEGINNER TO ADVANCED |
| 🚡 | 2 |
| ⬇ | 75% |
| ⬆ | 25% |
| 🕐 | 3–4 DAYS |
| 🧭 | NOT TOO BAD |

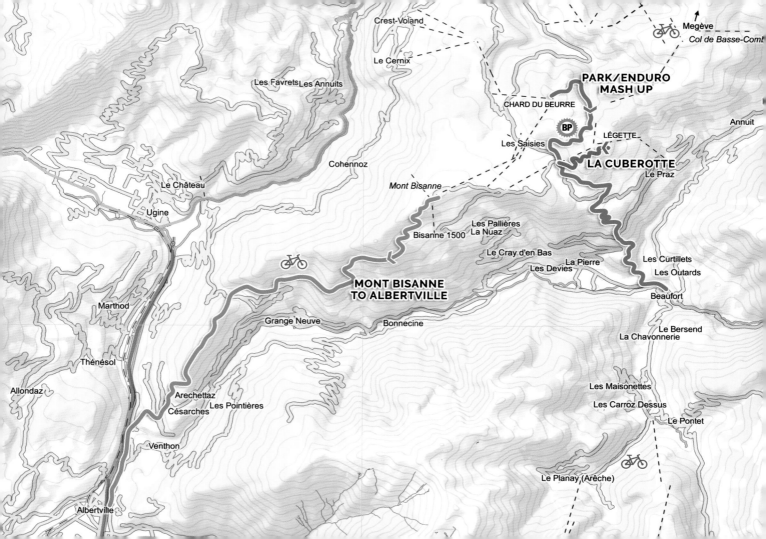

# Les Saisies

## Our pick

### MONT BISANNE TO ALBERTVILLE

Take the morning bus from the town up to Mont Bisanne and then charge down the forest ridgeline in a relentless pursuit of Albertville, over eighteen kilometres away. With a total vertical drop of nearly 2,000 metres, this is as big as anything in the Alps and mostly on untouched singletrack, deep in drifty loam. This is a marked route all the way to the valley floor, but, with several junctions along the way, I would highly recommend taking an IGN map with you. When you reach Albertville head for the Place de Mairie where a bus will take you back up to Les Saisies.

### PARK/ENDURO MASH UP

Head straight out the back of the Chard du Beurre lift to pick up a little-used singletrack that drops into some woods to the left. Take a right along the firetrack back to the Col de la Lézette before turning left just after the restaurant and hooking up with the blue trail back to the lift. Carry straight on and join up with the marked *Adret'Naline* line all the way to Beaufort. Catch the bus back to Saisies.

## Locals' choice

### LA CUBEROTTE

This black run off the Légette lift isn't the longest or gnarliest in the region, but the big doubles, north shore drops and gully gaps are a proper buzz, even for the most loopy of huckers. Long, easy approaches and smooth transitions mean a big DH rig isn't necessary to give them a go either.

## General info

The official site is a breath of fresh air for a French site, with all the information you need on the trails, ski lifts and bus links as well as some great videos of the park: www.sports-lessaisies.com
Or for the wider area have a look here: www.valdarly-montblanc.com

## Getting here

Les Saisies lies on the border between the Savoie and Haute-Savoie, around 30 kilometres from Albertville and within easy reach of Megève and La Clusaz if you're touring by car. Transfers from Geneva airport take about 1.5 hours and can be booked here: www.peaktransfer.com

# Les Saisies

## Town

It's fair to say that Les Saisies isn't the most rowdy place you'll ever visit. Sitting high on the mountain above Beaufort, near Albertville, the views are beautiful and the atmosphere very relaxed, but the limited nightlife and lack of amenities mean it's the town itself, rather than the trail network, that might make you want to move on after a few days. A handful of restaurants and bars will keep you going for a short stay though, while a trip into the valleys will get you a few supplies if you have a car.

## Lift dates

The lifts are open July and August, plus weekends at the end of June and early September. The buses which provide uplifts for the enduro routes run during the same period. The official site has all the info you need: **www.sports-lessaisies.com**

## Maps

A map can be bought at the tourist info for 2 Euros. For the long enduro lines out of the park you'll need the Megève IGN map – *3531 OT: Megève*. If you head right down into Albertville, *3432 ET: Albertville* might also come in handy.

## Where to stay

Camping Le Grand Tetras, which sits just below the main town, is worth it just for the views alone: **www.legrandtetras.fr**

Another good option is Hôtel Le Very on the main street which is very reasonably priced, ideal for lift access and has secure bike storage: **www.levery.net**

## Eating and drinking

The most popular spot on the main street is the Olympe Café, which has Wi-Fi, a friendly atmosphere and decent pizza. The Chalet des Marmottes just below the main street serves traditional local cuisine and does a great job of it.

## Bike spares

Sport 2000 on the main street has a few basic spares, mechanical support and Mondraker hire bikes. There's also an Intersport on the same street with Giant hire bikes available (Giant as in the make, not the size).

◀ Flat out through Alpine meadows en route to Albertville.

# Les Trois Vallées

Rocky, wild and untamed, this majestic landscape has big potential for epic enduro-style exploration. The ostentatious jet-set winter crowd aren't at all interested in the summer here and leave behind a deserted Alpine playground that anyone with a sense of adventure will adore.

## Introduction

To most of us, the likes of Courchevel and Méribel don't bring to mind images of an extreme environment. We tend to think of Gucci-clad snobs, more interested in their spa facilities than the scenery around them. This may be true of the winter, but summer reveals a rugged mountain of the old world. It's a remote and awe-inspiring place to ride, with Alpine singletracks winding off towards icy peaks and promising adventure at every turn. The area is huge too, covering all types of terrain from high-altitude rocky blasts to technical loamy woodland lower down. There are plenty of marked descents that would be fun on any machine, but to really get the most out of this place, arm yourself with a mid-travel trail bike and enjoy some classic Alpine riding: a bit of up, a lot of down, and a fair amount of everything in between.

## Trails

Although the area is one of the biggest names in the ski world, you might be surprised to see just how quiet the mountain is in the summer. You may spot a few other riders on the main lines into Méribel and Courchevel, but venture beyond these and a sense of complete isolation is easy to achieve, as if you've been riding for weeks to access the backcountry. Few lift-accessed resorts can offer this feeling of limitless adventure, and while there may not be too much in the way of freeride and north shore features, it can make the typical bike park look very sterile indeed.

But it's not just the quiet trails and big area that make this place great; there's also a huge variety of terrain to keep things interesting. Riding off the Saulire ridgeline into Courchevel, you'll encounter fast, rocky singletracks that drain incredibly well if the weather's not in your favour, while heading into the Méribel valley offers flowing hardpack descents in the style of a trail centre. Drop lower down towards La Tania or Brides-les-Bains and you're into a world of forest switchbacks and technical rooty lines. There really is something for everyone here. There's even a French Cup DH course into Les Menuires for those on a big rig, but be aware that the Saint-Martin lifts open only occasionally so it's not always an option to link with the other valleys.

In any case an enduro machine is easily burly enough to tackle most of the descents in the area, as well as letting you climb a little and explore all the great off-piste routes on offer.

INTERMEDIATE TO ADVANCED

10+

70%

30%

1 WEEK

NOT TOO BAD

◄ The fast and rocky singletrack of Courchevel.

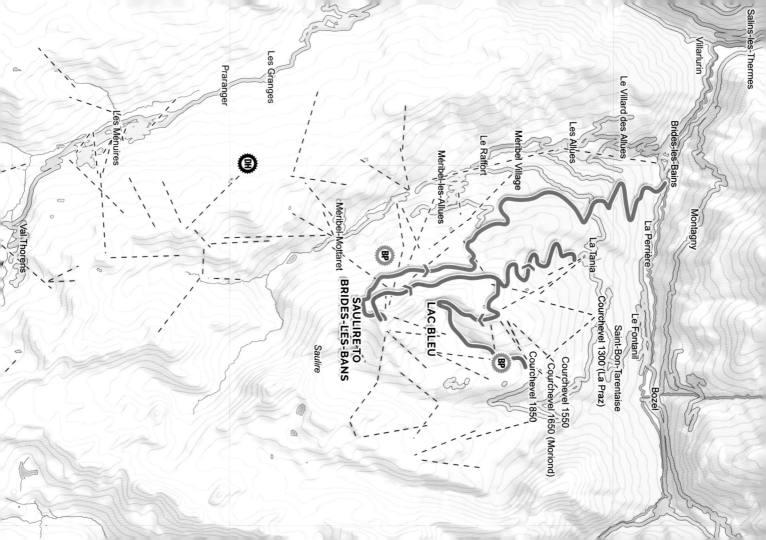

# Les Trois Vallées

## Our Pick

### SAULIRE TO BRIDES-LES-BAINS

With over 2, 000 metres of vertical descent, this route off the Saulire ridge is a big one! Take in the stunning views over the Vanoise glaciers before heading down towards Méribel along the black Saulire line. Pick up the fun and swoopy Bellevue traverse and then link up with the marked black trail that winds its way through the woods into Brides-les-Bains. A bus will take you back up to Méribel, but be sure to check the timetable.

### LAC BLEU

This small lake which sits above Courchevel is best reached by traversing and climbing along the firetracks above Méribel and below the Saulire ridgeline. From here there are some superb descents, either dropping north-east from the Col de la Loze through the technical forest into La Tania, or following a flat-out and stony singletrack back into Courchevel 1850 from the lake. Both are easy to spot once you reach the col.

## Locals' choice

The locals fly private jets and go to the opera. They don't ride pushbikes.

## General info

The official sites are next to useless and go some way to explaining why there's no one here. Merinet has far more information though, including trail maps and opening times: **www.merinet.com**

## Getting here

At around 1.5 hours from Grenoble airport by car, both Méribel and Courchevel are easy enough to access. There's also the option of taking a train to nearby Moûtiers, from where you can catch a bus or local taxi. Alpes Taxis offer transfers from Moûtiers and nearby airports as well as the nearby resorts of La Plagne and Les Arcs: **www.alpestaxistransports.com**

# Les Trois Vallées

## Town

There's the choice of all three valleys to use as a base, but the various Courchevel resorts represent the best option in terms of accommodation, nightlife and trail access. If you need to roll straight out on to the lift then Courchevel 1850 is the best bet, but if you don't mind a bit of a pedal then 1650 has more of a local vibe with reasonably priced eating, drinking and accommodation on offer. Avoid the Menuires valley as a place to stay because the linking lifts are rarely open, so you might just find yourself stuck there.

## Lift dates

From early July until the beginning of September. Again Merinet is the best place to find lift info: **www.merinet.com**

## Maps

A map can be obtained from the tourist info in Méribel or at the lift offices in Courchevel. You can also find it online: **www.merinet.com**

If you want more detail, get the IGN Top 25 map *3534 OT: Les Trois Vallées.*

## Where to stay

Courchevel 1650 offers the best deals in the summer. A good selection of apartments can found at Courchevel Chalet and Apartment rentals: **www.courchevel-chalets-apartments.com**

Méribel is also an option as a good central location for the trails: **www.meribel-chalets-apartments.com**

## Eating and drinking

There's not a whole lot going on in the summer but there's just about enough to keep you entertained for a week. Check out the Le Poste bar in Méribel where anyone of a biking inclination tends to flock after dark. The Bubble Bar in 1650 is a popular central hang out with free Wi-Fi and good food served all day. The Black Pearl is a little out of town in Saint-Bon-Tarentaise but serves amazing pizza with free delivery. They're particularly proud of their best review which simply states: 'Pizza anywhere else is pants.'

## Bike spares

Espace VTT next to the lift in Courchevel 1850 has Scott hire bikes and will carry out repairs.

# Leysin

World Cup heritage confirms the small but quality bike park at Leysin as a serious DH destination, while the lengthy and technical natural lines will feel like heaven for anyone looking for some epic Alpine enduro.

## Introduction

With some sensational vistas over the High Alps and Lake Geneva, the mountain resort of Leysin in the Vaud region of Switzerland offers some beautiful high-altitude riding both in and out of the well-designed park. The scope for exploring may not seem huge at first, but the funicular uplift from Aigle in the bottom of the valley means some monstrous descents can be had from the Berneuse lift, over 1,500 metres above. Don't mistake the backcountry as an excuse to break out your XC bike though, as the lines out here are steep, rocky and exposed, not to mention brutally long. A burly machine is a better choice and will let you take advantage of both the challenging features of the park and the technical enduro on offer.

## Trails

It's fair to say that with only one lift in operation and a less-than-inspiring trail map available, most riders won't exactly be salivating at the prospect of riding here. That's good news for the rest of us as you won't see another soul outside the park. Indeed, having spoken to various local riders hitting the DH runs, riders here seem utterly oblivious to the existence of any other riding in the area. To be fair, there are some fantastic creations in the park and if you're armed with a gravity-orientated machine you'll have a whale of a time charging through the rocky gullies before floating into town over the big doubles on the lower sections.

To me that's sort of missing the point though, as singletrack reigns supreme in Swiss riding and Leysin is no exception. From the lift you'll spot some glorious-looking lines picking their way down the jagged spine beneath you, and once you reach the Berneuse peak you'll discover that there are a whole lot more where they came from too, with ribbons of trails winding off though the meadows towards the hazy spectacle of Lake Geneva. Fun times lie ahead if you choose these lines, dropping towards Aigle at the bottom of the valley – but only if you're an accomplished rider. The gradient and exposure is quite sustained, and even the forest below presents a serious challenge with steep drops, tight switchbacks and some loopy freeride features built by the locals.

The marked XC routes attempt to imitate such adventures but they often fall short of the mark, sticking to firetracks and missing all the good bits. A much better idea is to arm yourself with a good map and make up your own itineraries utilising the big height drop from the Berneuse to Aigle. Remember the funicular isn't covered on the same pass though, so multiple laps of this big run can become pricey at 10 Euros per journey.

 **ENDURO/DOWNHILL**

 INTERMEDIATE TO ADVANCED

 1

 70%

 30%

 4–5 DAYS

 NOT TOO BAD

◀ Technical but great fun: Leysin off-piste.

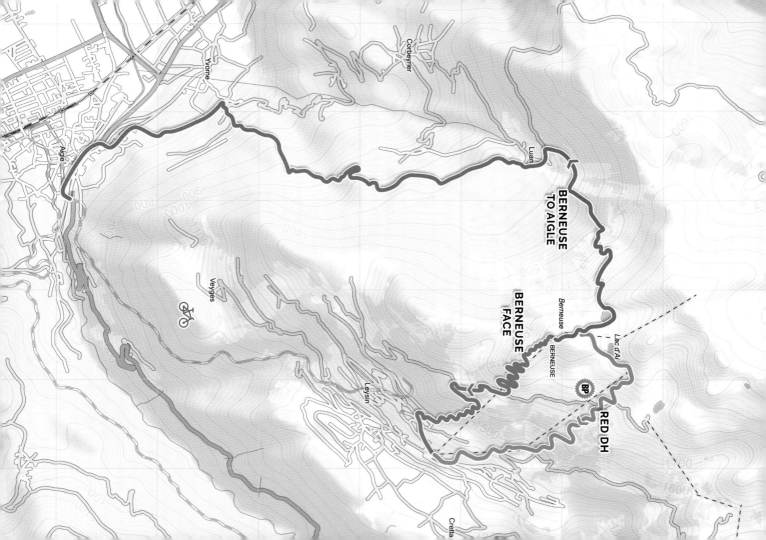

# Leysin

## Our pick

### BERNEUSE TO AIGLE

The big one! From the top of the Berneuse cable car follow the marked blue run and then cut left before the Lac d'Ai. At the col you'll spot the stony path winding down the grassy face and into the woods. Some of the turns are tight and off camber, requiring a steady pace, but as you head into the woods you can start to ease off the brakes and let loose into the village of Luan. From here, follow the signs to Aigle along a large firetrack before taking a small path to your right. This swoopy gully-run created by the locals is pure bliss, falling through the woods in water-chute style. Avoid the north shore features though, as they look to have been built a long, long time ago by someone who had totally lost their mind. Roll into Aigle, where you can catch the tram at a small station where the road starts to climb up to Leysin.

### RED DH

Most riders here are drawn like flies to s**t to the marked red descents from the Berneuse back into Leysin. You can see why, because they're fast and flowing with a good mix of roots, rocks and sandy sections. The bottom jump line works very well indeed and simply letting off the brakes will have you launching these things like Sam Hill on crack.

### BERNEUSE FACE

You can spot this line dropping right underneath the cable car and yes, it's as good as it looks, starting off with a very technical section over the rocky outcrops before opening up into a free-flowing lower section. The setting is truly Alpine, with magnificent panoramas over Mont Blanc and the Dents du Midi. At the Temeley farm, take the road for a couple of corners before swinging a left along the firetrack and then taking a right-hand turn after a couple of minutes. The snaking singletrack that criss-crosses this main line is a lot of fun, especially after a couple of laps when you really start to get your head around the insane levels of grip in the sandy loam. Follow your nose back into town when you hit the road.

## General info

The official site for the resort has information on opening times as well as a trail map for the park: **www.leysin.ch**

Also have a look at the Aigle website for information on the general area: **www.aigle-tourisme.ch**

## Getting here

Leysin is around 1.5 hours from Geneva, following the lake via Lausanne. You can also catch a train from Geneva to Aigle along the same route and then take the funicular up to Leysin: **www.cff.ch**

# Leysin

## Town

Sitting on a plateau above Aigle, Leysin is a typically posh Swiss affair complete with chocolate-box chalets and a revolving restaurant at the top of the mountain. The atmosphere is pleasantly laid back though and the town remains a vibrant spot throughout the summer, with a good selection of bars and restaurants to choose from. The linking funicular means the large town of Aigle (which is a simple train journey from Geneva) is also within easy reach. Here you'll find supermarkets, Chinese restaurants and local wine caves, so there's more than enough to keep you entertained for a few days.

## Lift dates

While the funicular from Aigle to Leysin runs for most of the year, you'll have to wait until mid-June to use the Berneuse cable car at Leysin. Be aware that you might encounter a fair bit of snow up top until late June. Like all Swiss resorts it's a long season though, opening until late October. Specific dates can be found at www.tele-leysin-lesmosses.ch.

## Maps

You can get a map of the park and some of the proposed XC trails at the Berneuse lift station in Leysin. Alternatively you can download it from the official site: www.leysin.ch.

To view hiking trails in the wider area, check out www.wanderland.ch

Irritatingly, the area is right on the spot between a few 1:25,000 maps. There's a fair bit on Swiss National map *1284: Monthey*, but you might want maps *1264*, *1265* or *1285*, depending on where you want to ride.

## Where to stay

There are a couple of good campsites in the area. Camping de la Piscine in Aigle has, as you may have guessed, a swimming pool: www.campingdelapiscine.ch. Camping du Soleil just below the main road into Leysin is an equally pleasant spot: +41 24 494 39 39.

## Eating and drinking

The Bel Air hotel can be found right next to the Berneuse lift, making it the perfect place to stay for getting straight out on the trails and for instant post ride refreshment in the bar: www.aubelair.ch

La Lorraine pizzeria in Leysin centre is a popular venue both for an afternoon beer and good feed in the evening. The Yeti bar and Club 94 are the best places to head if you're looking to get hammered with the locals.

## Bike spares

There are some good options in Leysin. Hefti Sports opposite the Berneuse lift has Scott hire bikes and a small selection of spares while Endless Ride just up the road is well worth a visit for local trail knowledge and mechanical support.

# Martigny

With year-round uplifts available courtesy of the super-efficient Swiss transport system, Martigny represents a great base from which to explore the magnificent Valais region and its network of world-class singletrack.

## Introduction

Bordering the French and Italian Alps, the Valais region of Switzerland is home to some of the biggest names in the business: Zermatt, Verbier and Saas-Fee. However, with so much bike-friendly transport available, it's possible to ignore the resorts altogether and really get inventive with your itineraries, which is where Martigny – the gateway to the Valais – comes in. The wealth of quality trails in this area would require a whole guidebook to itself, but basing yourself here can give a great introduction to what's on offer, taking advantage of the trusty PostBus, the local train and nearby gondola at Dorénaz.

## Trails

Helping you get the most out of the decent height gains in the area is the trusty PostBus that leaves from the town centre and takes you up to various destinations on the local slopes such as Chemin, Levron and the Col du Lein, from where you can ride glorious and pristine singletracks that drop back into the Val de Bagnes or into the town of Charrat just to the east of Martigny. Grip levels are high in the unmolested sandy loam, but some seriously exposed and steep lines mean you do have to be of a good level to enjoy it. Verbier is also easily accessible via the train to Le Châble, but far more in keeping with our backcountry vibe is to head to Orsières instead and then take the bus up to the Col du Grand-Saint-Bernard, where forgotten tracks sneak through the shale and rocky outcrops back towards the valley and give a proper 'out there' feel.

Other options include taking the bus up to the Col de la Forclaz and sampling some of the eastern sections of the Tour du Mont Blanc, or taking the Mont Blanc express train up to the French border where a whole other valley full of technical, rocky singletracks will deliver you back into the Valais.

The possibilities don't end there either, as just 20 minutes' pedal to the north lies the small town of Dorénaz and its gondola that gives year-round access to some fast and adrenaline-filled descents with jumps, drops and berms built into the natural lines to create a park-like feel.

Still not enough? Then how about a short train journey north to Bex (page 247), where you can hop on the funicular to Villars and drift down the wildly addictive natural and locally built lines in the sunny, wooded slopes.

With so much variety, the local terrain around Martigny is an enduro heaven that should be high on the list of any skilled and adventurous rider.

---

**DOWNHILL/ENDURO/XC**

| | |
|---|---|
| ○–● | INTERMEDIATE TO ADVANCED |
| 🚡 | 1 GONDOLA PLUS BUS/TRAIN |
| ⬇ | 70% |
| ⬆ | 30% |
| 🕐 | 3–4 DAYS |
| ⊘ | TRICKY |

---

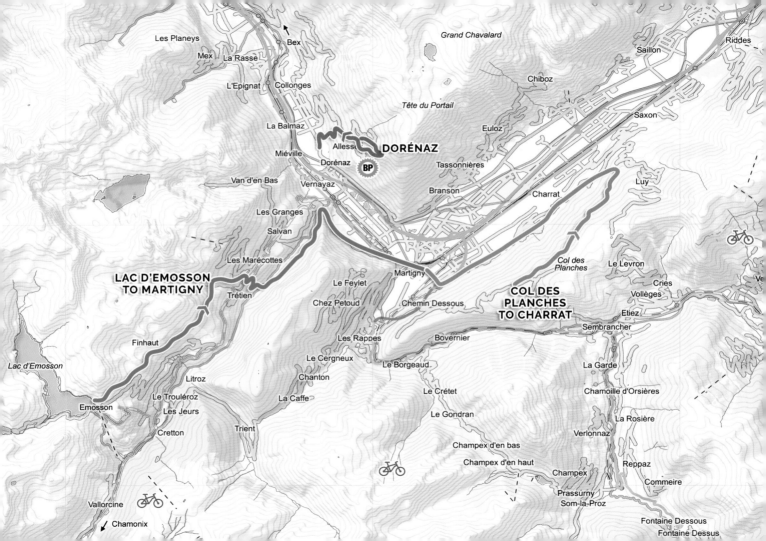

Les Planeys

Bex

Mex

La Rasse

L'Epignat

Collonges

Grand Chavalard

Saillon

Riddes

Chiboz

Saxon

Tête du Portail

La Balmaz

Alless

DORÉNAZ

Miéville

Dorénaz

**BP**

Euloz

Luy

Van d'en Bas

Vernayaz

Tassonnières

Branson

Charrat

Col des
Planches

Le Levron

Les Granges

Salvan

**LAC D'EMOSSON
TO MARTIGNY**

Les Marécottes

Trétien

Le Feylet

Martigny

Chez Petoud

Chemin Dessous

**COL DES
PLANCHES
TO CHARRAT**

Cries

Vollèges

Etiez

Sembrancher

Finhaut

Les Rappes

Bovernier

Le Cergneux

Le Borgeaud

La Garde

Lac d'Emosson

Litroz

Chanton

Le Crétet

Chamoille d'Orsières

Le Trouléroz

Les Jeurs

La Caffe

Le Gondran

La Rosière

Cretton

Emosson

Trient

Verlonnaz

Reppaz

Champex d'en bas

Vallorcine

Champex d'en haut

Champex

Commeire

Chamonix

Prassurny
Som-la-Proz

Fontaine Dessous

Fontaine Dessus

# Martigny

## Our pick

### LAC D'EMOSSON TO MARTIGNY

The spectacular Lac d'Emosson sits high above the Vallorcine valley and marks the trail head for one humongous descent into Martigny.

Take the Mont Blanc express train up to Finhaut and then a bus up to the incredible feat of engineering that is the Lac d'Emosson reservoir. Look for a small rocky track that cuts up above the main parking area and heads east above the main road to Finhaut. Rocky is the only way to describe this magnificent and wild track that gently descends and traverses across the face towards Trétien. It's properly tricky stuff and almost trials-like in sections, but persevere because as you drop further into the valley the rock gives way to deep forest loam and the trail really picks up speed. As you drop through countless switchbacks through Trétien and down to the river you get a strong sensation of a descent that will never, ever end. Alas it does, but by the time you reach Martigny after an hour's singletrack descent of 1,500 vertical metres, you won't feel hard done by.

### DORÉNAZ

With two dedicated downhill runs that are served all year round by a small gondola, the little-known village of Dorénaz is a favourite amongst local DH chaps. The descents are way more singletrack than bike park, but the numerous drops and small jumps built into the sandy trails provide great flow. If hardcore enduro is still on the mind then consider climbing out of the lift and up to the Tête du Portail above.

From here you can cut across the face of the Grand Chavalard along a skinny and terrifying line that redefines the term 'exposed'. Descend through Chiboz and Euloz for a nerve-settling beer back in the village.

### COL DES PLANCHES TO CHARRAT

Catch the bus up to the village of Chemin and then pedal up the road towards the Col des Planches. Before you reach the top you should spot a firetrack to your left which leads to Le Planard. Head straight on and you'll pick up a long and challenging singletrack that hugs the side of the mountain and threatens to drop you into the valley below at every switchback and exposed traverse. It's technical stuff but fast and fun too, with huge grip in the untouched loam of the forest floor. Things get pretty lairy lower down as the trail starts to open out and you can exploit the terrain even further, getting off the brakes entirely and weaving through the pines at loopy speeds.

The trail criss-crosses a firetrack before doubling back and dropping through the vineyards into Charrat, from where you can cruise along the lane to Martigny.

# Martigny

## General info

For general information on Martigny and the local valleys have a look at the official tourism site: **www.martigny.com**

The local park at Dorénaz has a dedicated Facebook page where you can see the latest news and videos of the trails: **www.facebook.com/DorenazBikePark**

## Getting here

Whether you're flying into Geneva or driving as part of a multi-point tour, Martigny is easy to reach. You can catch a train direct from Geneva airport which takes around 1.5 hours or drive here in about 2 hours via Lausanne and Montreux. It's also not too far from Chamonix via the Col de la Forclaz (50 minutes by car) and within reach of Italy and Pila/Aosta via the Col de Grand-Saint-Bernard (1 hour 15 minutes by car).

Train times and prices from Geneva: **www.cff.ch**

## Town

Martigny has always been an important cultural and trading centre, with transport links to Italy, Chamonix, Lake Geneva and eastern Switzerland. This is great news for us biker folk who see only uplift opportunities as opposed to a slick public transport system, but it's also influenced the city and you'll find a surprisingly cosmopolitan vibe here with a wide range of eateries, bars and entertainment sitting side by side with ancient Roman heritage. The city prides itself as an arts centre, so you can get reckless in the mountains before soaking up a bit of culture and local wine as the sun goes down.

## Lift dates

The area offers a huge season for riding with uplift opportunities all year round, so you can get up there as soon as the snow has melted. For specific times of the Dorénaz lift have a look on their site here: **tinyurl.com/dorenaz-lift**

For times and dates of the train and PostBus see their respective sites here: **www.cff.ch** and here: **www.postbus.ch**

For the Finhaut to Lac d'Emosson bus see here: **www.sbb.ch**

◀ Typical Valais – rocky up top, wooded lower down – Col des Planches.

# Martigny

## Maps

A great start for any of the Swiss trails is the Wanderland site, where you can type in your area to bring up an OS/IGN-style map with all the marked trails highlighted: **www.wanderland.ch**

Another great site for route ideas around Martigny and the wider Swiss area is Biking Spots, which gives you a map and detailed itinerary of suggested rides: **www.bikingspots.ch**

This is a big area, so you're looking at a lot of maps. A good place to start might be **www.map.geo.admin.ch** which lets you view maps at whatever scale you want. After that go to **www.swisstopo.admin.ch** and find the 'National Map 1:25,000' interactive grid to work out which maps you need.

## Where to stay

Camping Les Neuvilles is a tranquil spot but still close to the city centre and Roman amphitheatre, so is well worth checking out if you have your own transport.

The Hôtel du Stand is also a good choice in the centre, with clean rooms and helpful staff: **www.hoteldustand.ch**

## Eating and drinking

After charging through the vineyards all day you'll almost certainly want to sample some of the local produce. There are numerous cellars throughout the centre but the Florian Besse cave at the foot of the Forclaz vines is an authentic venue where the hosts will help you get lashed in a cultured fashion. Don't expect any raucous pubs either, this is an arts centre with a proud history remember, so sophisticated wine bars are the order of the day. La Vache qui Vole is a suitably posh bar and restaurant serving gourmet dishes Swiss style, while the incredibly authentic and delicious Chinese dishes at Kwong Ming are testament to the diversity on offer in Martigny.

## Bike spares

You'll find Bike'n Joy on the main street through the centre. It's not a huge shop but they have a good range of spares and accessories and can offer mechanical support.

◀ Enduro on an epic scale – Lac d'Emosson.

# Megève

Often overlooked in favour of nearby Chamonix, Megève has the views, the trails and the lift network to provide proper Alpine enduro on an epic scale. From gentle woodland cruising to steep, technical and full-throttle charging, everyone will find something they love in this undiscovered MTB playground.

## Introduction

Those that come to Megève with full-on downhill insanity in mind will probably go away disappointed. There are a few berms and north shore features dotted throughout the woods, but if you're looking to roll out of the lift and hit the park all day then there are better places. Megève is more about big mountain enduro and hunting out pristine forest singletrack by using lifts and leg work in equal measure. It's a hugely satisfying place to explore too, because those sweet trails are literally everywhere, deep in loam and seemingly never-before ridden.

The lift system covers a large area of varying terrain and gradients, so you really can go as big, steep and exhausting as you like, making Megève a great place for anyone wanting to push their limits, no matter what their ability, in a backcountry, rather than park, environment.

## Trails

At first glance the trail map looks nothing short of vast, with marked itineraries stretching hundreds of miles. Most of that you can ignore though, especially the routes dropping into the Sallanches valley as it's mostly just psychopath XC stuff that only Euro types with heart rate monitors and diet plans will enjoy. Instead, focus on the lift-accessed zone west of Combloux, which includes the Megève, Praz-sur-Arly and La Giettaz areas. This is still a huge expanse to explore, covering several valleys and mountain faces that all offer something a little different.

The Jaillet woodlands above Megève are by far the most popular and it's here that most effort has been put into trail building. Long, sweeping turns and mellow gradients characterise the man-made descents into Megève and Combloux, which are great for beginners as they give an introduction to the steep Alpine forests in a controlled and safe environment. But head towards the ridgeline beyond this area and things get a lot more exciting as you pop out of the treeline on to one of the most stunning Alpine traverses around, with Mont Blanc on one side and the Aravis range on the other. There's a feeling of limitless possibility up here as woodlands and valleys stretch out before you, all of which contain virgin forest singletrack just begging to be ridden.

Choose from either dropping back into the Jaillet area, exploring the wilderness into the Torraz valley to the north, or descending all the way down to Praz-sur-Arly and the steeper, more technical trails there. Just remember there's a whole lot more than the route guide would suggest, so get a decent map and keep an eye out for the good stuff.

BEGINNER TO ADVANCED

3

65%

35%

1 WEEK

NOT TOO BAD

◄ Drifting through the brown pow – Christomet trail.

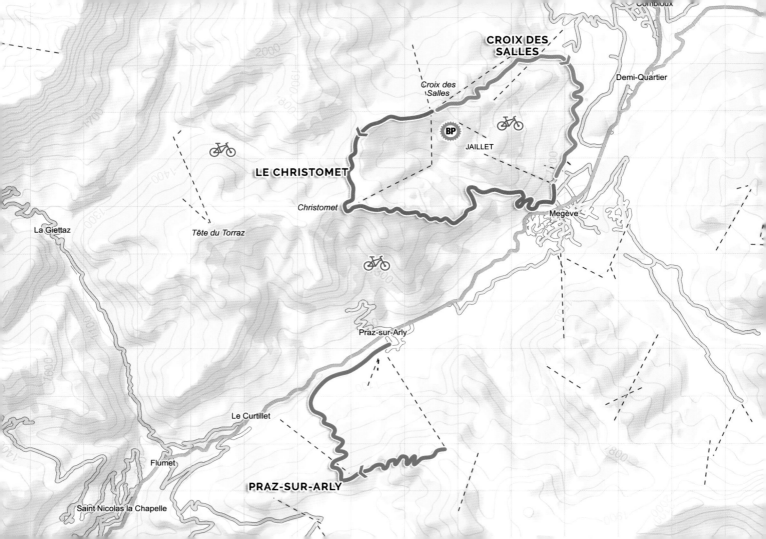

# Megève

## Our pick

### LE CHRISTOMET

From the top of the Pertuis chairlift, drop down the ridgeline, ignoring all the junctions, and climb up to the Christomet peak straight ahead of you. The views from the top are magnificent, but you'll have little interest in them once you spot the glorious singletrack that sits on top of the spine in front of you. The loam and pine needles are so deep that you have the sensation of floating through the trees. The 'brown pow' continues all the way into the meadows below, where you can cross the river and head back to Megève.

### PRAZ-SUR-ARLY

The lift at Praz-sur-Arly is best accessed via a descent from the Torraz or Christomet peak. Try not to follow the marked descents from the top, but instead look for the secret lines that criss-cross them. With steep gullies and rooty drops, they're a little steeper and more technical than those on the other side, but brilliant fun if you've got the confidence to hit them fast.

## Locals' choice

### CROIX DES SALLES

This peak above Megève marks the trailhead for most of the man-made descents in the area. Once you know the forests into the Jaillet and Combloux woods, you can really start to mix up your favourite bits of bike park and natural trail. The gentle gradients mean beginners can build their confidence without the risk of a horrific death, whilst more competent riders can get off the brakes and charge.

## General info

For basic information on the area check out the official website: www.megeve.com or for the wider area have a look here: www.valdarly-montblanc.com

## Getting here

Megève is part of Portes du Mont Blanc ski system, easily reached from Geneva airport (just over an hour) or from Chamonix (40 minutes). A minibus transfer can be arranged through Megevexpress: www.megevexpress.com

# Megève

## Town

Megève is a large winter resort, sitting at mid-altitude just above the valley linking Geneva and Chamonix. It has the feel of a large town rather than a quaint mountain village, but it's still a pleasant spot and what it may lack in cow bells and cuckoo clocks it more than makes up for in post-ride entertainment and amenities. There's a swimming pool, bowling alley, fancy bars and even a McDonald's for when you really can't be arsed.

As with any ski station in the summer there are many accommodation options at reasonable prices, from camping to swanky apartments and five-star hotels.

## Lift dates

Generally the lifts run from early July until early September. Specific times and dates can be found here: www.megeve.com

## Maps

You can get hold of a trail map at the Jaillet lift or online at: www.valdarly-montblanc.com

IGN map *3531 OT: Megève* covers much of the riding, although you might sneak onto *3430 ET: La Clusaz/Grand-Bornand*, depending on how far north you ride.

## Where to stay

Camping la Demi-Lune is a little way out of town but has easy access to and from the Jaillet lift by bike: www.camping-lademilune.com

If you're looking to go a little more upmarket then Hôtel les Cimes in the centre offers a warm and friendly service (as long as you're not too covered in crap). The Healthy Holiday Company offer guided holidays in the area if you're after an all-in-one package: www.thehealthyholidaycompany.co.uk

## Eating and drinking

There's a lot of choice here but if it's the local cuisine you want then Restaurant Le Savoyard will oblige with a life-threatening cheese fest that will have you sweating pure camembert for weeks afterwards. Some good burgers are on offer here too so avoid McDonald's and head to OK Burger, because while it may have the most underwhelming name ever, it can rustle up a delicious burger and home-made chips.

Le Jazzy's is a popular bar that often has live music in the high season while club Palo Alto goes on into the small hours if you hate riding sober.

## Bike spares

Bike Addict has a range of Kona hire bikes as well as local guides and some basic spares: www.bike-addict-megeve.com

# Montgenèvre

Sitting high on the Italian/French border, the town of Montgenèvre is home to some of the most amazing singletracks you're ever likely to encounter. Add to this the sandy, flowing DH runs of the bike park and you have one of the most varied and underrated riding spots in the Alps that riders of all abilities can enjoy.

## Introduction

Montgenèvre is one of the few riding spots here that really offers something for everyone. Most of the trails in the bike park only drop around 400 metres on smooth, sandy terrain, so it's a great place to experience Alpine riding for the first time without fear of dying horribly in the first turn. The black-graded routes also have plenty of north shore drops and rock gardens thrown in, adding more difficulty but still maintaining the glorious flow that these gentle slopes offer. It's not all about the bike park though, with some stunning high-mountain enduro that's easily accessible from the lifts. These backcountry singletracks are good, so good in fact that I can't possibly do them justice with mere words – they need to be ridden to be believed.

Montgenèvre is easily reached from nearby Sauze d'Oulx or Serre Chevalier and could easily be ridden on the same trip.

## Trails

The bike park itself is to be found under the Chalmettes and Gondrans lifts, with a good range of green to black runs that makes it ideal for those wanting to progress during their holiday. Much like the nearby resorts of Serre Chevalier and Sauze d'Oulx, the park has a definite fun, rather than extreme, feel to it. This is in part due to the shallow gradient of the mountains here and the sparse, open woodlands, but it's also down to the design of the trails. They utilise the terrain much like the UK trail centres, keeping height and allowing you to roll through the natural features without having to hang on the brakes.

You'll see plenty of full-on DH rigs rolling out of the lifts, but they're not really necessary. A big enduro machine will handle everything here and allow you to explore the fantastic singletrack away from the park.

To do that, use the Gondrans lift, ignore the marked runs and head into the backcountry. It's big mountain riding at its best along shaley, hard-packed trails that hug the side of the peaks and offer spectacular views all around. The terrain up here verges on desert scrubland and, with many abandoned forts along the ridgelines, really feels quite exotic to ride through. Big enduro loops are possible over the border into Italy, rolling effortlessly along smooth singletrack back into the town. Equally good stuff is to be found on the other side of the valley, off the Chalvet lift, with endless drifts through the pine needles of the Rocher Diseur.

There's also the possibility of some big descents, dropping into Briançon from the Fort de l'Infernet and taking the navette (bus) back to town. Plenty of scope then for a week of great riding on almost guaranteed dry trails.

 BEGINNER TO ADVANCED

 3

70%

30%

4–5 DAYS

NOT TOO BAD

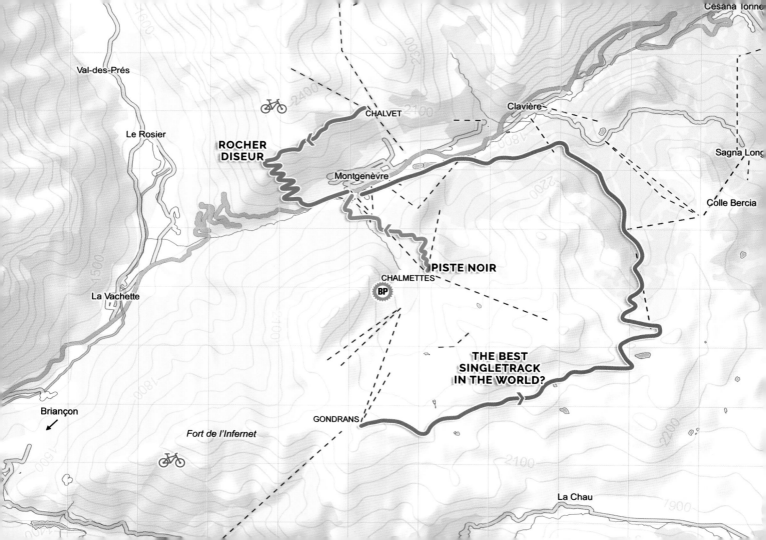

Cesana Torine

Val-des-Prés

Le Rosier

CHALVET

ROCHER
DISEUR

Clavière

Sagna Long

Montgenèvre

Colle Bercia

PISTE NOIR

CHALMETTES

BP

La Vachette

THE BEST
SINGLETRACK
IN THE WORLD?

Briançon

Fort de l'Infernet

GONDRANS

La Chau

# Montgenèvre

## Our pick

### THE BEST SINGLETRACK IN THE WORLD?

From the top of the Gondrans lift, head flat out down the ridge towards Italy. Traverse around the back of the Chenaillet and Charvia peaks, taking in the stunning vistas over the Italian valleys. Cut left above the Lac Gignoux and climb up over the col and across the border. Dropping right behind the ridge, pick up a trail winding down through the valley on the left. Heading back towards the town, the singletrack is simply perfect and by far and away the best I've ever ridden. It's very fast, very long and the word 'flow' doesn't even come close.

### ROCHER DISEUR

From the top of the Chalvet lift, take a left and cruise along the rocky trail towards the Rocher Diseur. From this mini peak the views through the valley back to Briançon are awesome, and so is the trail that drops back down to the col. A series of endless switchbacks become very addictive and you'll almost certainly want to hit this a few times. When you reach the main road there's a 10-minute climb back up into the town.

## Locals' choice

### PISTE NOIR

The black run from the Chalmettes lift is a great descent that uses the fast and dusty terrain to full effect, with medium-sized hits built in all the right places to keep the trail flowing and add some decent air time.

## General info

The bike park has its own half-arsed website with very little information on anything at all: tinyurl.com/montgenevre-bikepark

General info on the resort can also be found at tinyurl.com/montgenevre-resort

## Getting here

The closest airport is Turin, which is around 1 hour 10 minutes away by car. It's not far from Briançon either, so a train and then taxi transfer is also an option. Transfers from there or from Turin and Grenoble airports can be booked through the Alpine Transfer Company: www.alpine-transfer-company.com

# Montgenèvre

## Town

The town lies on top of the Col de Montgenèvre and feels very much in the heart of the mountains. Although fairly quiet in the summer, a mixture of French and Italian culture makes for a surprisingly cosmopolitan vibe and a good variety of cuisine. It also results in a ridiculous local accent that sounds very much like a hammered Frenchman – of course this might actually be the case.

The location makes it great for exploring the nearby Alpi Bike resorts in Italy as well as Briançon and its associated forts on the French side.

## Lift dates

Getting hold of lift information is like getting blood out of a stone, but generally speaking July to early September is a good bet. You can try and extract information from the defensive staff on (+33) 492 21 52 52.

## Maps

A map can be obtained from the lift caisse or online from: tinyurl.com/montgenevre-bikepark

1:25,000 scale IGN map *3536 OT: Briançon* should stop you getting lost.

## Where to stay

There's a lot of empty ski accommodation to choose from here. Go Montgenèvre offers a good range of apartments, both catered and non-catered: **www.go-montgenevre.com**

## Eating and drinking

It's not exactly kicking off here in the evenings but it's not totally dead either. There's a good variety of cuisine thanks to the location. Le Transalpin serves top notch and authentic Italian dishes, while Le Refuge fights the French corner very well. Pizza joints are everywhere.

Le Graal café has a good atmosphere and free Wi-Fi. You can stay here too for just 50 Euros B&B.

## Bike spares

There are a few shops here catering for most basic spares and repairs. Sport 2000 has Commençal hire bikes and a fair selection of parts. Skiset also has a few bits and pieces as well as some dodgy hire bikes if you fancy something that rides terribly.

# Pila and Aosta

With huge height drops and a world cup track on offer, Pila is hard to beat if you're armed with a big rig and a craving for extremely long descents. The natural stuff is also some of the best in the Alps, putting Pila high on the bucket list for any gravity-oriented rider.

## Introduction

Pila sits high on the mountain above the beautiful Aosta valley in northern Italy. It's not far at all from Chamonix, but the riding couldn't be more different. Here the terrain is gentle, sandy and sparsely wooded, which lends itself to trails that really charge down the mountain rather than pick their way down steep and technical lines. This is definitely true of the bike park and its famous 'freeride' track into Aosta, but even the natural singletrack has a swoopy flow to it that allows you to get off the brakes and attack.

That's not to say it's easy though. Both the man-made and natural trails are very rewarding for a confident rider, but beginners will find the length and intensity of the descents, as well as the riders around them, just too intimidating.

## Trails

Taking the long cable car from Aosta up to the resort of Pila, you'll catch glimpses of a fun-looking trail dipping in and out of the pines and cutting through the vineyards on the lower slopes. This is the so-called 'freeride' trail, which at eight kilometres long is a huge draw to the area. It's easy to see why, with long drifting turns, gullies and drops providing a roller-coaster sensation all the way from Pila to the valley floor.

Save that one for later and jump on the second lift which gives you access to the main park. This is where you'll find the world cup track, complete with original starting gate and gangs of Sam Hill wannabes.

It's a good fun course that doesn't require top-level skills to ride, even if it is at a slower pace than the pros. Several similar tracks can be found in these woods, all featuring high banked turns and varying sizes of jumps and drops. One of the best can be found off the Couis 1 lift which is only open on certain days. Make the most of it if you get up there and link up with the lower freeride trail to give a hefty 2,000-metre height drop – all on hand-built trails.

It's when you head out of the park though that the real magic happens. None of it's shown on the trail map, but a little exploring will reveal a hidden network of superb singletrack, particularly from the Lago di Chamolé – just a small pedal above the Chamolé lift – where you'll discover ridgelines that are nothing short of spectacular. From the lake you can either carry on climbing up to the magnificent ridgeline trail described below in 'Our pick', or just descend straight from the lake along some very fun, fast-rolling singletrack that snakes through the forest parallel to the main park runs. There are a few options here, but whichever you pick should eventually bring you to a large path which traverses back to the Chamolé lift, so you can't go far wrong.

Avoid anything you find here marked 'XC' though, which will lead you on a mind-numbing tour of the local firetrack.

**DOWNHILL/ENDURO**

| | |
|---|---|
| ⬤-⬤ | INTERMEDIATE TO ADVANCED |
| 🏛 | 3 |
| ⬇ | 90% |
| ⬆ | 10% |
| 🕐 | 5 DAYS |
| 🧭 | NOT TOO BAD |

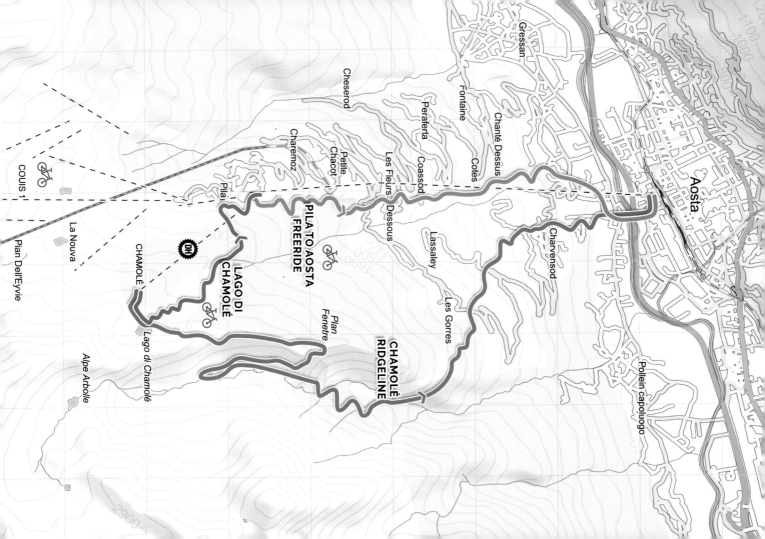

# Pila and Aosta

## Our pick

### CHAMOLÉ RIDGELINE

From the top of the Chamolé lift, climb to the lake and then continue up to the Col d'Arbolle. This beautiful ridge-top trail leads you right alongside the cliff edge before snaking down towards the Plan Fenetre. At this point take a right and double back on yourself, picking up a swoopy track underneath the rock face. Cruise down through the valley until you get a chance to cross the river. As the firetrack brings you back on to the main face, spot a singletrack off to the right which switchbacks through sand and loam all the way to Charvensod and the valley floor.

### LAGO DI CHAMOLÉ

Again, climb to the lake above the Chamolé lift, but this time drop to the left and pick up a winding ribbon of singletrack through the meadows and rocky outcrops. The trail sneaks into the pines below and brings you out on to the lower section of the blue run in the park. Finish up on the massive bermed line into the finish area.

## Locals' choice

### PILA TO AOSTA FREERIDE

You would have to be dead inside not to enjoy this huge adrenaline rush from Pila to the valley floor. Big sandy berms, drops, hips and flat-out sections make this giant descent an absolute riot. Several options on the way down keep things interesting, but it's so long you would never get bored of it anyway.

## General info

The official tourist website has some basic info on the park including a map and lift opening dates: tinyurl.com/pila-info

## Getting here

Aosta is about an hour's drive from Chamonix through the tunnel. If you're flying then Turin airport is the closest. From here you can take a train or transfer to Aosta and Pila: **www.trenitalia.com** and **www.airporttransfers.it**

# Pila and Aosta

## Town

Pila may give immediate access to the bike park at the top of the mountain, but Aosta is the better option if you're staying for a longer period. It's not only great to finish the day with a huge descent into the valley, but the city of Aosta offers way more in terms of nightlife and general amenities. The old town is a buzzing regional centre complete with markets, street acts and much of its Roman heritage still on display. It provides a unique opportunity to soak up some proper Italian culture whilst completely covered in shit.

## Lift dates

The lifts are open from late June until mid-September. Dates and times can be found at: tinyurl.com/pila-info

## Maps

A trail map is available at the Pila-Aosta cable car or at the Chamolé chairlift. Get hold of the Italian IGC 1:50,000 scale map number 3: *Il Parco Nazionale Gran Paradiso* for a more detailed look.

## Where to stay

Two tranquil campsites are located not too far from the Aosta lift and a large supermarket: **www.campingtouring.com** and **www.campingmontebianco.it**

If you would rather be in the centre then there are many hotels to choose from. A nice mid-range option is the HB Aosta hotel located at the western edge of the old town. The rooms aren't huge, but they're modern, well equipped and have fantastic views over the old town and the Pila mountainside: **www.hbaostahotel.com**

Les Arcs isn't too far away either and some bike-specific chalets offer tours here: **www.whiteroomchalet.com**

## Eating and drinking

The main square is a great place to chill, soak up the atmosphere and enjoy a pizza and a Peroni. There are so many options here but local favourites include the Gekoo, complete with a bar fashioned from a VW camper, and La Dolce Vite, where you can sample the finest Aosta wines and hams like a proper snob.

Also check out Pizzeria Moderno just beyond the western end of the main square to soak up the hectic and amusing atmosphere created by the animated staff and demanding clientele – the food is great too!

## Bike spares

The MTL rental centre is located at the bottom of the Chamolé lift. There's a range of random bikes available as well as some basic spares and a mechanic to carry out some repairs if you ask nicely.

◄ Singletrack all the way to the valley floor – Lago di Chamolé.

# Portes
# du Soleil
overview

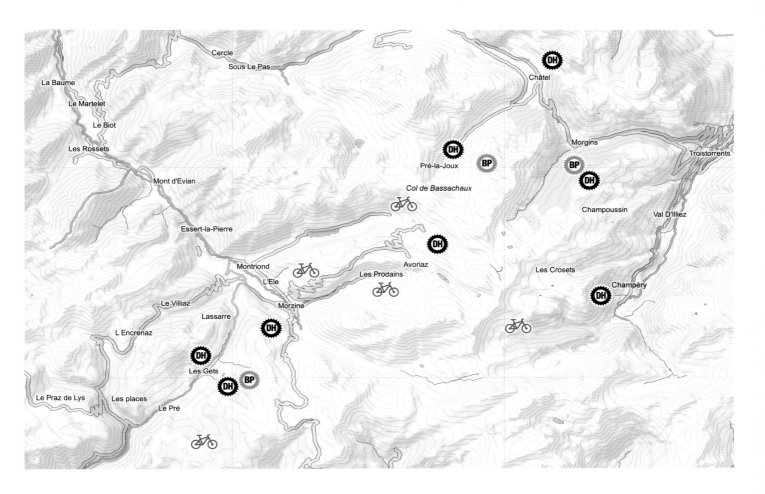

La Baume

Le Martelet

Le Biot

Les Rossets

Cercle

Sous Le Pas

Châtel

Mont d'Evian

Pré-la-Joux

Morgins

Troistorrents

Col de Bassachaux

Champoussin

Val D'Illiez

Essert-la-Pierre

Avoriaz

Les Crosets

Montriond

Les Prodains

Champéry

L'Ele

Le Villiaz

Morzine

Lassarre

L Encrenaz

Les Gets

Le Praz de Lys

Les places

Le Pré

# Portes du Soleil overview

The Portes du Soleil needs little introduction. One of the original bike parks, it's still hugely popular and remains the best known of all the European destinations.

Although there are many new parks on the scene, all claiming to be bigger and better, there's a reason that riders flock here by the thousands each summer. Mainly it's the sheer size. Over twenty lifts operate during the peak months, meaning riders can cover a huge region with minimal pedalling. Nowhere in the Alps offers such an extensive system of man-made trails and bike-focused infrastructure, with many shops, events, bars and accommodation all aimed squarely at the mountain biker.

There are of course the much-talked-about downsides, namely braking bumps. These do become savage by mid-season, especially on the main lines in Les Gets and Morzine, but this is true of any major bike park in the Alps.

What sets the area apart from other parks, such as Les Deux Alpes or Tignes, is the scope for exploring the natural trails away from the crowds. There are no restrictions on bikes in the region, adding a great feeling of adventure and variety which some other big-name destinations can lack.

Officially the system is made up of twelve resorts. That's a bit of a red herring though, as many of those don't have lifts and can't really be linked without a lot of effort. For this guide we've divided the area into three distinct zones:

## Les Gets and Morzine

The big ones. This is where the majority of riders end up staying. As well as having the most runs, they're easy to access from Geneva, which is just an hour away, and have many deals on accommodation, transfers and catering. They also have the best après-bike vibe and there's no shortage of like-minded folk to share a beer with.

## Champéry and Morgins

The Swiss side of the Portes du Soleil has a whole different feel again and the trails can feel totally empty in comparison. Being the hardest to reach if you're coming from the UK, the area can feel a little bit exclusive and has a much longer season. Some top-notch enduro and a world cup track can often be had all to yourself.

## Châtel and Avoriaz

Right in the heart of the system, they're a little harder to get to and as a result are quieter and more chilled. Châtel is the clear freeride zone in the system and possibly the whole of Europe, with a lot of work having gone into the big north shore style features.

◀ Photo: John Coefield

# Portes du Soleil overview

## General info

You can find a good basic overview of the area on the official site, with links to accommodation, events and lift opening dates: tinyurl.com/portesdusoleil-biking

## Getting here

The PdS is a huge area spanning France and Switzerland, so getting here will depend largely on where you choose to stay. Generally speaking though, you'll be looking at flights into Geneva and then a taxi transfer or drive up to the resorts. Les Gets and Morzine are just over an hour's drive, while Châtel, Morgins and Champéry will take an extra 30 to 45 minutes. Go Massif and Ski Lifts are your best bet for airport transfers. It's worth considering the super-efficient Swiss trains if you're heading to Champéry: **www.sbb.ch/en**, **www.gomassif.com** and **www.ski-lifts.com**

## Lift dates

Normally the lifts run every day from mid-June to mid-September, but it does vary between resorts. Les Gets tends to get its season going earlier than others, often opening from mid-May (weekends only), whereas Champéry – like much of Switzerland – stays open far later, usually well into October. You can check the individual dates for each resort here: tinyurl.com/portesdusoleil-lift

## Where to stay

The PdS is still the most popular biking destination in the Alps and that means there's no shortage of accommodation, especially in Morzine and Les Gets, where there's something to suit every budget. Some of the best include Riders Refuge in Morzine and Le Boomerang hotel in Les Gets. The Swiss resorts are typically pricey in comparison but both Morgins and Champéry have some good camping options which are popular among bikers: Camping la Mare au Diable and Camping du Grand Paradis. See the individual sections for more information.

## Eating

Like most mountain resorts you can expect a lot of cheese in various melted states to dominate the menus. It's impossible to differentiate between any of these sorts of places so just take your pick. There are some international options available too, especially in Les Gets where you can tuck into a curry at the Bombay Ski Club or some fish and chips at Le Boomerang. There are some decent bars to be found, all brimming with fellow riders/weirdos willing to talk biking nonsense with you. Some of the most popular include Chez Roger in Morzine and the Avalanche and Nazca bars in Châtel. Again, see the individual pages.

## Bike shops

This is definitely one of the better mountain resorts for bike spares, with many ski-turned-bike-shops hoping to snare their captive audience with a myriad of the latest shiny things on display. From the well-stocked Nevada Sports in Les Gets to the imaginatively named Bikeshop in Champéry, you should find enough mechanical support to keep you going for a week.

◄ Switch off the brain and hit the berms – Nauchets, Les Gets.

# Les Gets and Morzine (Portes du Soleil)

As the true origin of the Alpine bike park phenomenon, Les Gets and Morzine are some of the biggest names in the business. The area has lost none of its appeal either, with huge numbers still drawn to the massive network of trails, biker-oriented accommodation and easy access from Geneva.

## Introduction

Even without the rest of the Portes Du Soleil system on tap, the area of Morzine and Les Gets is pretty extensive, with countless runs on offer and more appearing every year to cope with the thousands that ride them. Although there's no big mountain stuff here, it has everything the gravity-fed bike park warrior could wish for – a huge number of graded descents from ultra-mellow greens to black-graded jump parks, a solid network of lifts, an equally solid network of burger bars and very little in the way of culture. The forever-sold-out Pass'Portes du Soleil event which starts and finishes here is further evidence of the popularity the area still has. The downsides of this are clear: during the peak season the br(e)aking bumps become so savage it's close to unbearable, while shock bush and frame bearing sales go through the roof.

## Trails

The southern side of the Les Gets valley is littered with tracks hacked into the mountain and development shows no sign of slowing down. This is particularly true of the Nauchets area, which has the most recent stuff and remains in relatively good condition with fun and heavily bermed descents. The jump park has now been moved here too, for easier access to cart away the bodies. It features some decent drops and wall rides and is good fun for the confident rider. With shaley trails, it drains well and rarely becomes super slippery like the muddy Morzine side.

Although many will argue that main lines like the *Chavannes* are great, avoid them like the plague if you have any sort of dignity or like your bike – they're brutal fights on destroyed and largely featureless trails. Yes they're a challenge, but more in the style of battling against a terrible illness than of a great descent.

If it's singletrack you're after, throw the bike map away and head for the woodlands of Morzine, which are home to some beautiful loamy riding. None of it's particularly official, but there are some superb lines on either side of the main *Pleney* run which are great fun if you're not freaked out by steep gradients and technical rooty sections. There's similar stuff on the opposite side of the valley, west of the Super Morzine lift, which is easy to spot if you head along the main firetrack above the lift and then follow your nose to Morzine. Some of the sections, especially those that utilise the natural gullies, really are fantastic, but are best avoided in the wet unless you're into the whole steep-and-off-camber greasy root scene.

Also worth checking out are the marked XC routes across the Plateau de Loëx, which can be accessed from the Nauchets lift. The pedal up to this beautiful woodland puts most riders off, but there are some great singletrack descents to be found. The technical but gloriously flowing trail from the creepy Chapelle de Jacquicourt is an absolute must if you make it up here.

In fact with no restrictions on biking there really is a lot to be found that isn't on the map. It adds a little bit of adventure that some other parks with big claims lack.

| | |
|---|---|
| ●–● | BEGINNER TO ADVANCED |
| 🎫 | 7 |
| ⬇ | 90% |
| ⬆ | 10% |
| 🕐 | 1 WEEK |
| ⊘ | EASY |

◄ Cheeky singletracks can be found all over the mountain – Nauchets, Les Gets.

LES GETS AND MORZINE (PORTES DU SOLEIL)  **155**

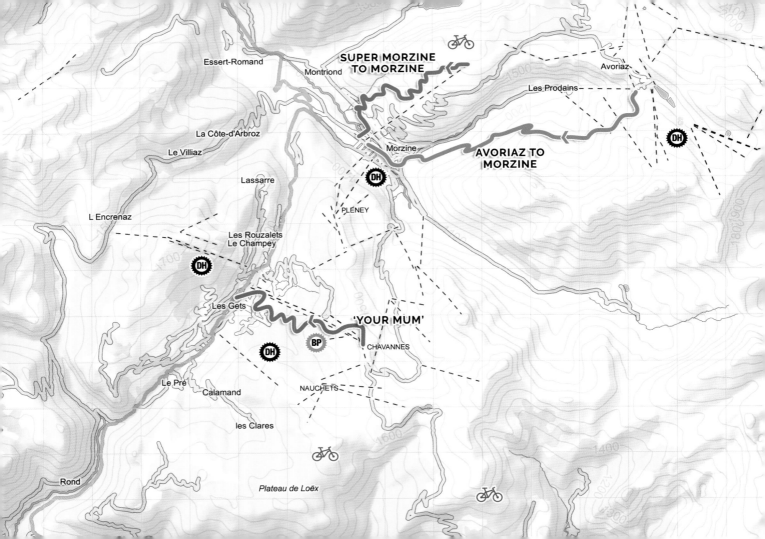

# Les Gets and Morzine (Portes du Soleil)

## Our pick

### SUPER MORZINE TO MORZINE

If you're going to build a bike park track then this is how to do it. Dropping into the red run from the Zore chairlift above Morzine, you're instantly into a sizeable road gap and then on to wonderfully flowing berms and endless tabletops that just work so well. Take a right above the Super Morzine télécabine and pick up any one of the brilliant secret singletracks through the woods down into the valley. It makes for a great mash up of natural and man-made riding, and is very typical of what's on offer here.

### AVORIAZ TO MORZINE

A brilliant enduro loop away from the park. From the top of the Prodains lift at Avoriaz, take a right and climb up the ridge in front of you heading for La Chaux. A panoramic traverse brings you to the small hamlet of Morzinette where the fun really begins. One of the fastest singletracks you'll ever ride, it sweeps through the forest on a gentle gradient and drops you back into Morzine centre.

## Locals' choice

### 'YOUR MUM'

A secret line off the *Chavannes* run, this is a good fun singletrack that is super popular with the locals, though I suspect mostly because of the name. No one ever tires of telling one another 'I rode your mum today', 'I saw someone go down on your mum earlier' ... You get the idea. Stay away after the rain though, as your mum is a filthy mess in the wet.

## General info

Les Gets has quite a good site of its own with plenty of pictures and videos of the trails: **en.lesgets.com/mtb**

For all the information on linking resorts including the individual lift dates, have a look at the Portes du Soleil site: **tinyurl.com/portesdusoleil-biking**

## Getting here

Les Gets and Morzine are easily reached from Geneva airport via car and are only around an hour or so away. There are also many transfer companies such as Go Massif (**www.gomassif.com**) or Ski-Lifts (**www.ski-lifts.com**), who can take you there by minibus.

## Town

Les Gets is overrun with bikers during the summer months, making it a great place for meeting fellow riders. There's something of a 'lads on tour' atmosphere here, and there's always someone to argue with on the topics of trails, component choice and who is the most attractive girl in the bakery.

Morzine has more of a typical Alpine feel, with plenty of cuckoo clock chalets, cheese shops and cow-orientated souvenirs on offer. It's still very much a biking venue though and you'll find no shortage of nightlife and like-minded folk to hook up with.

# Les Gets and Morzine (Portes du Soleil)

## Lift dates
Les Gets tends to open a little earlier than the rest, from weekends in mid-May onwards. The whole area is up and running from mid-June to early September. All the dates can be found here: tinyurl.com/portesdusoleil-lift

## Maps
A map can be obtained from the lift caisse at Morzine or Les Gets and you can also download them online at tinyurl.com/portesdusoleil-bikemap

You won't need a map if you're on the marked runs, but *3528 ET: Morzine* covers the area. If you plan on exploring far to the south of Les Gets, get *3530 ET: Samoëns* too.

## Where to stay
There are so many options it's hard to single anything out. Riders Refuge offer lots of options in Morzine including package deals with transfers and lift passes included: www.ridersrefuge.co.uk/summer

Accommodation in Les Gets can be found here on the Les Gets site: tinyurl.com/lesgets-accommodation

## Eating and drinking
Nightlife in both Morzine and Les Gets is pretty good and very mountain bike-orientated during the peak season. Le Boomerang is a classic in Les Gets and shows the world cups live on the big screen.

With a loyal seasonnaire following, the Cavern in Morzine is as close to a UK nightclub as you'll find in the Alps.

Burgers and fondues are everywhere and you'll have no trouble spotting them on a wander through the main streets.

## Bike spares
Les Gets has plenty of shops with probably the best range of spares you'll find anywhere in the Alps (one of the upsides to the large numbers who come here) and some good deals can be had towards the end of the season. Nevada Sports is one of the best with many models of brake pads, mechs and clothing available. It also rents Specialized bikes at a not-too-ridiculous rate. The best bet in Morzine is at Torico which has a decent amount of spares, mechanical knowledge and Nukeproof hire bikes.

◄ North shore the way it should be ridden. Les Gets bike park.

# Champéry and Morgins (Portes du Soleil)

The Swiss resorts of Champéry and Morgins receive way fewer visitors than the French side of the PdS and make for a more chilled-out base to explore this well-known system. A world cup DH course as well as some fantastic backcountry enduro ensures plenty of trail choice too.

## Introduction

Officially there are four resorts on the Swiss side of the PdS, but, in truth, Les Crosets and Champoussin can be grouped into the Champéry system, so we'll talk about this area in terms of Champéry and Morgins. Champéry is the hub here, not least because it hosts a round of the world cup most years. It's far from busy though and the trails are much quieter than Les Gets and Morzine. It's far wilder than you might expect from the PdS, with some adventurous enduro loops away from the masses under the magnificent peaks of the Dents du Midi.

Linked to the Portes du Soleil via some stunning mountain passes, this is one of the few spots in the system where you can get that all-important big-mountain feel, something that's generally lacking in the rest of the area.

## Trails

The area goes under the name of 'Swiss bike park', and while it may be linked to them, it really does have a whole different feel to the likes of Morzine and Les Gets. The trails are far quieter and don't receive the same levels of abuse as the French side.

Many riders will have had their only taste of riding here during the Pass'Portes du Soleil event, when thousands arrive to cause carnage on the trails. That's a shame because while they're fighting to get ahead of the slow guy in front they've totally missed the adventurous appeal

of this normally quiet side of the mountain. Make the trip over here at any other time and you're greeted by a breathtaking backdrop of huge jagged peaks which give the trails a wild and epic feel.

Most of the marked runs are up high above the treeline and drop into the Crosets valley just above Champéry. Although a lot of fun for all levels, there's nothing too serious and most of the trails can be tackled by an intermediate rider. It's hard-packed and drains well too, so it's good all-weather stuff. The same can't be said of the world cup course lower down in the woods. Like all the trails on this steep-sided woodland it's technical, rooty and downright scary in the wet, leaving anyone but expert riders a nervous wreck. Morgins is properly DH-focused but the flowing turns and berms linking heavily rooted sections provide something for all abilities.

It's not all about the bike park though. Some brilliant 'off the map' enduro is to be found here as well, particularly off the Col de Cou, where you'll find pristine and untouched singletrack – something you wouldn't normally associate with the Portes du Soleil.

  INTERMEDIATE TO ADVANCED

 5

 80%

 20%

 1 WEEK

 NOT TOO BAD

◀ Swoopy bliss on the Col de Cou trail.

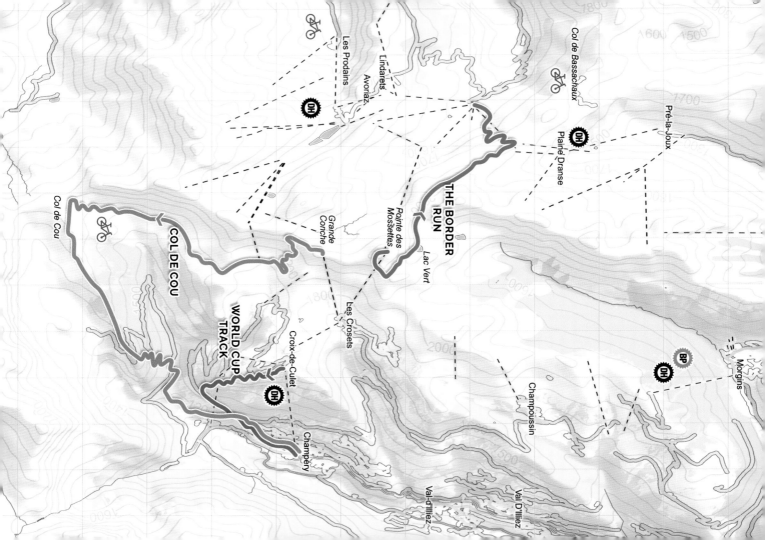

# Champéry and Morgins (Portes du Soleil)

## Our pick

### COL DE COU

From the Pointe des Mossettes, head south down the ridgeline and take the marked black trail towards Les Crosets. When you hit the firetrack, take a right and follow it as it traverses round the valley and climbs towards the Col de Cou. Just before the summit you'll spot a singletrack leading back towards the town. This smooth, fast and immensely fun line with backdrops over the Dents du Midi is simply stunning, and right up there on the must-do Alpine list.

### THE BORDER RUN

For a big day out from the French side, take the lift to the Pointe des Mossettes and then swing around the peak, heading back into France. Take a left at the col and drop down singletrack to the Lac Vert. Climbing gently over another col, the trail then becomes a flat-out blast on a high mountain line into the Lindarets valley. Pick up the red marked descent to the Lindarets lift, from where you can take a lift back to the Morzine valley.

## Locals' choice

### WORLD CUP TRACK

Even the pros don't make this one look easy, and riding it for yourself it's easy to see why. Very steep and technical, it takes some real balls to launch down this thing like you see them do in the World Champs. Get a few corners hooked up and you'll feel like king of the world, don't and you'll quickly find out how good (and expensive) the Swiss health system is. A genuine DH classic marked from the top of the Croix-de-Culet lift.

## General info

The bike park has its own website which does a great job of making the area look truly awful: **www.bikepark.ch**

No less frustrating, but with a lot more information, including all the individual lift dates, is the Portes du Soleil site: **tinyurl.com/portesdusoleil-biking**

## Getting here

Morgins and Champéry are the furthest resorts of the PdS to reach by car if you're coming from the UK. Although not far by bike from Morzine and Les Gets, they're at least another 40 minutes' drive through the Abondance valley. A good option is to get the train here from Geneva. Times and prices can be found here: **www.sbb.ch**

# Champéry and Morgins (Portes du Soleil)

## Town

With the most stunning backdrops in the Portes du Soleil and very steep terrain, Champéry feels much more extreme than its French counterparts, and proper 'heart of the mountains' stuff. The town itself isn't exactly quaint as you might expect from a Swiss village, but if it's this you're after then Morgins most certainly is, with a proper cow-and-meadow vibe.

Champéry has plenty of bars and restaurants to choose from and a long lift season open into mid-October. It's all at reassuringly high Swiss prices however and a little harder to reach than the French side if you're coming from Britain.

## Lift dates

Like most of the Swiss parks, the area stays open much later than its French counterparts, especially Champéry, whose main Gondola runs well into October. If you're looking to link with the rest of the system then mid-June to early September is a good bet. All the dates can be found at: tinyurl.com/portesdusoleil-lift

## Maps

A map can be obtained from the lift caisse at Morgins or Champéry. Like the rest of the PdS the marked runs are easy to find and the Morzine IGN map (*3528 ET: Morzine*) covers most of the off-piste stuff. You could add Swiss National Map *1304: Val-d'Illiez* if you wanted to head further east.

## Where to stay

For something laid back, check out the camping at Morgins, Camping la Mare au Diable, or at Champéry, Camping du Grand Paradis.

Hotels are fairly pricey around these parts but there are a few budget options such as the Backpacker Le Petit Baroudeur situated near the station. You can sneak your bike into a bunk bed if no one's watching.

## Eating and drinking

There's no shortage of extortionately priced restaurants on offer in Champéry, but they're often top-notch. The food at the Hôtel Le National is proper fine dining. There are also some good value options if you have a look around. Le Farinet Restaurant & Nightclub has a decent atmosphere, pizza and occasional live bands. La Crevasse bar has a real nice vibe and live music during peak season.

## Bike spares

The best bet here is the self-titled Bikeshop underneath the main cabin in Champéry. It has a reasonable selection of spares and Scott hire bikes at very unreasonable prices.

◄ Man just cannot beat nature – Col de Cou.

# Châtel and Avoriaz (Portes du Soleil)

Sitting right in the heart of the system, Châtel has earned a reputation as the most extreme spot in the Portes du Soleil. Huge north shore hucks and regular freeride events typify the area, but there's also some great trail riding to be done in the adjoining Avoriaz and Lindarets valleys.

## Introduction

Many riders' only taste of this area will have been during the Pass'Portes du Soleil enduro event. Most of them look wide-eyed and terrified, recounting tales of the crazy obstacles on view. Indeed as you drop into the Châtel valley from Morzine, you'll notice massive north shore drops built into the hillside. Don't worry, these aren't part of the red run, but the course for the Châtel Mountain Style, a freeride event in the style of the Redbull Rampage. Although not quite as ridiculous, the marked black trails do feature some serious stuff and it really is the place to be if getting airborne is your thing.

Despite this, the area has worked hard on building trails for all levels, with many lines being reworked to be fun for all abilities. It's not all bike park either and many enduro lines can be sought out with a little exploring.

## Trails

Most of the riding in Châtel actually takes place quite a way up the valley in the Pré-la-Joux area – there is a bus running from the town to the lift for bikers. In fact the trails are easier to access via Avoriaz and Morzine and that's the way most riders will have come.

Dropping straight into the blacks with all those big features built in, you immediately understand where Châtel's reputation for advanced freeride comes from. It's not the whole story though, and the locals work harder than most to ensure that the runs not only stay in good condition, but appeal to all levels of rider.

Alex Evans, who is a key member of the trail team, gives the lowdown – from the horse's mouth, so to speak: 'Châtel's increased popularity has meant that trail development and maintenance have been at the forefront of the bike patrol's priorities. For 2014, there is a remake of an old track called *Haute-Tension* (high tension), which is a red. This track was inspired by the idea of not having to brake whilst losing altitude by hitting berm after berm, that change in rhythm, to get you down the hill with a massive grin on your face.'

If the grin starts to fade then the Lindarets valley adds a bit more adventure with some great backcountry singletrack. The Lindarets valley is a bit of a hidden gem in this respect, with many swoopy and natural-feeling descents on the Avoriaz side. You can also find some untouched, wiggly singletracks in the forests west of the Col de Bassachaux that link back to the Lindarets lifts (see 'Our pick'). Also worth checking out is the trail from Avoriaz into Morzine via Morzinette (see the Les Gets and Morzine section). This is proper off-the-beaten-path stuff and not the sort of thing you expect from the PdS, but as with the other resorts here, there's a lot of scope outside the park.

BEGINNER TO ADVANCED

6

90%

10%

1 WEEK

EASY

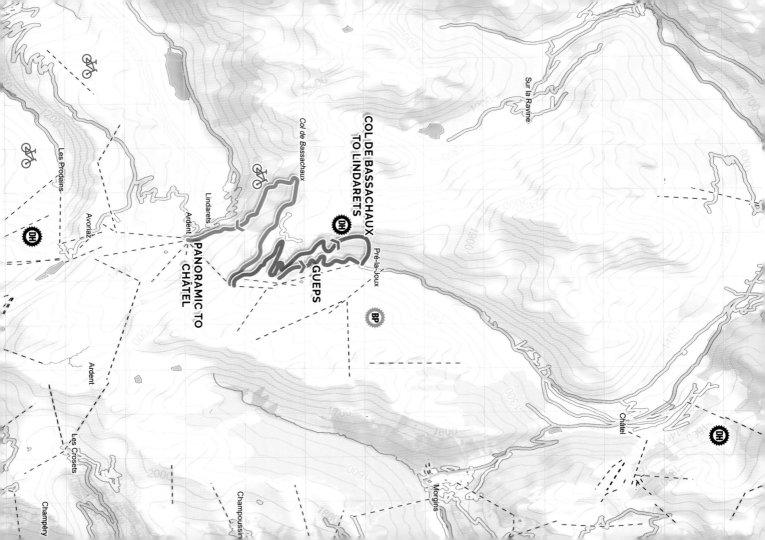

# Châtel and Avoriaz (Portes du Soleil)

## Our pick
### PANORAMIC TO CHÂTEL

It's often the case in bike parks that the green runs can be the most fun, largely because peer pressure to hit the black stuff leaves them untouched and fast rolling. Châtel is no exception and the *Panoramic* trail is a hoot. A long sweeping line off the Rochassons lift, it has been reworked with constant rollers, humps and bumps that make it a blast no matter what level you are.

### COL DE BASSACHAUX TO LINDARETS

A fantastic and often-overlooked enduro line from the top of the Chaux Fleurie lift. Climb up to the Tête de Lindarets before picking up a beautiful flowing singletrack passing through the Col de Bassachaux. Keep rolling all the way to the steep rock faces of the Pointe de la Chavache. Take a left and the fun continues all the way back to the Lindarets lift.

## Locals' choice
### GUEPS

More local wisdom from my horse on the inside, Mr Evans: 'My personal favourite is the *Gueps* black trail that starts off with some jumps into the open, but quickly plunges into the forest with technical corners, roots and drops. At the end of the track you can either join the *Ric et Rac* (a red with more jumps), or make your way on to the scary black with huge jumps called *Zougouloukata*.'

## General info

Châtel has a good site with plenty of information on the park at:
**tinyurl.com/chatel-biking**

As with all PdS resorts some general info can be found at:
**tinyurl.com/portesdusoleil-biking**

## Getting here

Châtel is a little harder to get to than Les Gets and Morzine, another 35 minutes' drive through the Abondance valley. If you don't fancy driving then you can get a minibus transfer through Professional Transfers:
**www.professionaltransfers.com**

# Châtel and Avoriaz (Portes du Soleil)

## Town

Châtel is one of the most picturesque and traditional Alpine towns you're likely to come across. Partly because of its beautiful Alpine setting, but mostly because the majority of the riding and the filthy idiots that go with it are kept at arm's length further up the valley. The same can't be said of Avoriaz, which is one of the most dire and depressing places to stay during the summer months – the design having clearly been chosen to reflect a nuclear fallout zone. It does serve as a good link between the other valleys though and access to the trails is very good.

It's a little harder to link Châtel with the other resorts, but it would definitely be the better place to stay. With a chilled-out rather than rowdy atmosphere, it's ideal after a day of balls-out charging in the park.

## Lift dates

From weekends in mid-June and full time from end of June to early September: tinyurl.com/portesdusoleil-lift

## Maps

A map can be obtained from the tourist info in Châtel or at the Pré-la-Joux. You can also download them online from: tinyurl.com/chatel-info

For detail, look for *IGN 3528 ET: Morzine*.

## Where to stay

There are many hotels in Châtel. A good value option is Le Choucas near the bus pick up and Super Châtel lift: **tinyurl.com/choucashotel**

If you're looking for something self-catered then check out Chalet Group Châtel: **www.chaletgroupchatel.co.uk**

## Eating and drinking

Up on the mountain you'll find yourself drawn towards La Perdrix Blanche at Pré-la-Joux. It's not a bad choice actually, with good grub served on the terrace. Back in town Le Vieux Four serves delicious food in a traditional setting.

Châtel doesn't exactly kick off in the evenings but the Pub L'Avalanche has a nice vibe to it with occasional live bands

## Bike spares

Twinner has a few spares knocking about, as well as Scott hire bikes. With some random bits and pieces for sale and GT hire bikes, Switch 5 is also worth checking out.

# Saint-Luc

Perched high in the giddy, vertical world of the Anniviers valley, Saint-Luc offers quintessential Swiss singletrack set against seriously stunning backdrops. A small but hardcore park adds some adrenaline to the mix.

## Introduction

Saint-Luc isn't an obvious choice in this area. Nearby Zermatt has the most famous backdrops and singletracks in the business, while Crans-Montana in the Sierre valley below boasts an established park scene. In truth though, the riding at Saint-Luc is every bit as good, both in the park and out in the wilds. The funicular uplift is open much earlier than its neighbours, and the sunny slopes mean dry and dusty trails by early spring, so you can get your big-mountain singletrack fix before the main biking season really kicks off.

Like most of Switzerland the bus service throughout the area is regular and reliable, so you can link to other resorts in the valley and create some huge descents in the process. Big hits and awkward drops mean the park is no beginners' zone, but many of the smooth and flowing natural lines can be enjoyed by most abilities and are equally stunning whether you're flat out or just cruising.

## Trails

Saint-Luc is one of a handful of resorts in Anniviers valley, alongside nearby Chandolin, Zinal and Grimentz. All have lifts running during the summer, but Saint-Luc boasts the best and most easily accessed trails, along with a much longer season of uplifts courtesy of the funicular. It's also the only resort here with a bike park and it's very popular with the locals, who session the large freeride features built into the red and black routes. Even the blue run is fairly tricky, so there isn't much

here for timid riders, but the sandy conditions and big hits are a hoot for anyone looking to be either in the air or in a wild drift for the entire length of their run.

The funicular takes you from the town at 1,700 metres to Tignousa at 2,200 metres, so we're not talking massive height gains, but the best stuff (as with most of the Swiss resorts) is to be found by grabbing your trail bike and climbing beyond the lift into the wilderness. Many of the best lines start from the Hôtel Weisshorn, either snaking through the gorse or dropping steeply through deep loam in the woods towards La Combaz, from where you can cruise back along the road into Saint-Luc. It's a bit of a slog up firetrack to the hotel, but the rewards are definitely worth it as breathtaking singletracks wind off towards the glaciers beyond.

The lift at nearby Chandolin is also worth checking out (when it opens, a little later in the season) as it gives you access to technical, rocky singletracks and very long and steep descents into the Sierre valley below. This is a very real option, as a bus links all the resorts and can carry you back to the town from wherever you end up, but be warned that this is a pricey service and will cost upwards of 15 Euros each time.

| ENDURO/DOWNHILL | |
|---|---|
|  | INTERMEDIATE TO ADVANCED |
|  | 2 |
|  | 60% |
|  | 40% |
|  | 3–4 DAYS |
|  | NOT TOO BAD |

◀ There are plenty of jaw dropping singletracks from the Hôtel Weisshorn.

SAINT-LUC  **173**

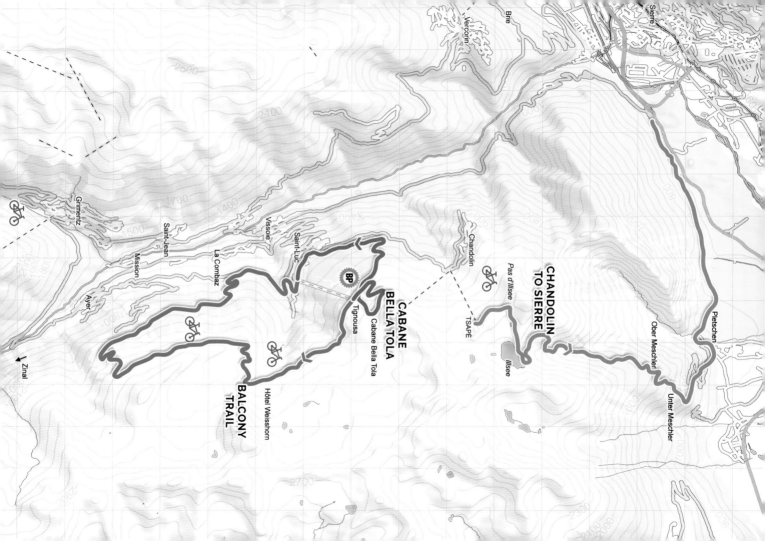

CHANDOLIN TO SIERRE

CABANE BELLA TOLA

BP

Cabane Bella Tola

Tignousa

BALCONY TRAIL

Hôtel Weisshorn

Saint-Luc

Vissoié

La Combaz

Saint-Jean

Mission

Ayer

Grimentz

Zinal

Chandolin

Pas d'Illsee

Illsee

TSAPÉ

Vercorin

Brie

Sierre

Ober Meschler

Unter Meschler

Pletschen

2500

2100

1700

1400

1500

1800

1000

2700

2300

2900

# Saint-Luc

## Our pick
### CABANE BELLA TOLA

Take a left out of the Tignousa funicular and climb up to the Cabane Bella Tola. Just past the cabin you'll spot a sweet-looking trail undulating through low-lying gorse back towards the funicular. This trail is so smooth and fast that you'd be forgiven for thinking it's part of a park, with only the lack of braking bumps giving it away. Once you hit the firetrack, take a right turn and then the left-hand fork before picking up a singletrack on your left. This forest line is nothing short of incredible, floating over a deep bed of pine needles on a gentle gradient in a relentless pursuit of speed. Follow your nose back into town.

### BALCONY TRAIL

From the top of the funicular follow the signs to the Hôtel Weisshorn. It's not a particularly exciting climb up the firetrack, but the views up towards the Weisshorn and Bishorn are staggering. Once you reach the hotel, climb up to your left and on to the balcony trail heading towards Zinal. Big-mountain singletracks don't get any more epic than this, with the rocky terrain and huge glaciers beyond making you believe you're in the middle of the Himalaya. Continue along this line until you see a small track on your right zigzagging through the meadows and on to a firetrack. After a couple of corners take a right turn, following signs for Saint-Luc. This lovely rolling singletrack is so thick with deep red pine needles that it's like riding along a big soft ginger beard. When you reach the small chalets take a left and drop down through the forest to La Combaz before cruising back along the road into Saint-Luc.

## Locals' choice
### CHANDOLIN TO SIERRE

Locals talk in romantic tones with misty eyes about the descent from Chandolin to the Sierre valley, and with good reason. It's big one, starting from the top of the Tsapé lift at Chandolin and then climbing up to the Pas d'Illsee, where a descent of almost 2,000 vertical metres awaits. From here you head down to the Illsee reservoir on a rocky singletrack and then drop down below it, swinging wide around the bowl to the west before cutting back across the gorge and then traversing around the eastern side of the valley through the hamlets of Ober and Unter Meschler. Glorious forest switchbacks drop you all the way to the valley at Pletschen, where you can cross the river, heading west, and charge through the gently undulating Pfynwald woods and back to the road junction for the Val d'Anniviers. You can catch a bus here back up to Saint-Luc and a well-earned beer. **Make sure you have an adequate map and check bus and train timetables before setting off.**

# Saint-Luc

## General info

The bike park has its own dedicated site with information on opening dates, prices and a map of the park: **www.bikepark-stluc.ch**

For information on riding in the wider area have a look at the Anniviers valley site, which gives some route ideas and the specific maps you need to follow them: **www.valdanniviers.ch**

## Getting here

Although it's possible to get here via train and bus from Geneva, you're better off with your own transport if you're just here for a few days. Heading along the lake from the airport via Martigny will take around 2.5 hours, but of course there are many places to stop en route, including Verbier, Leysin and Crans-Montana.

If you do get the train to Sierre, or get adventurous with your routes, then you'll need to know the times of the PostBus which runs throughout the area. **www.postbus.ch**

## Town

The small resort of Saint-Luc is built on the most preposterously steep slopes you can imagine, so negotiating your way around on foot is exhausting, and downright sketchy if you've had a few pints. Luckily the central area is quite compact, and there are only a handful of restaurants and bars open in the summer, so there's no need to stray too far. The upside to such a location is that the views of the high, snowy peaks are amazing and make for a pleasant spot to relax after a hard day's riding

## Lift dates

The funicular at Saint-Luc is open from the end of May, while the other resorts in the valley usually open from July onwards. For specific times and dates see the general Anniviers site: **www.rma.ch**

◀ Singletrack, Swiss style – the Balcony trail.

# Saint-Luc

## Maps

A map of the park is available at the funicular, but for all the natural trails you'll need a proper map. A number are available for the Anniviers region – you want Swiss National Map *1307: Vissoie* for the immediate area, adding *1287: Sierre* for the trails down into the valley.

## Where to stay

The Hôtel Beausite has clean, comfortable rooms, helpful staff and great views over the valley: **www.lebeausite.ch**

Another good option is the Camping d'Anniviers in the town of Vissoie lower down the valley. From here you can take a bus or drive up to Saint-Luc, which takes around 15 minutes. **www.camping-anniviers.ch**

## Eating and drinking

A popular venue is the Fougère bar and pizzeria not far from the funicular. It's a lazy spot where locals play cards and bikers drink beer after a day's riding. The food is tasty and there's the option of a basic but clean and friendly B&B too. **www.hotelrestaurantlafougere.com**

## Bike spares

There's a small hire point at the funicular itself with a random selection of bikes and very basic selection of spares so make sure you bring everything you need!

◄ Good trails, great views – this is how the Swiss do singletrack. Above Saint-Luc.

# Salève

Just a stone's throw from Geneva airport, the Salève is probably the most easily accessible Alpine destination from the UK. It's very good too, with long swoopy descents to rival anything in the High Alps, as well as stunning views over Lake Geneva.

## Introduction

You've probably never heard of this place, but if you've driven into the Alps from Geneva, chances are you will have passed by it. On arrival, watching the gondola climb over the motorway to the top of a severe-looking rock face, Salève doesn't appear to be the most obvious place for bike trails. However, the scene at the top is quite different, with Alpine pastures and gentle wooded slopes providing the perfect landscape for fast and swooping singletrack. Not content with that, the locals have done a huge amount of trail building, adding berms, big jumps and creating adrenaline-filled lines out of the natural terrain. The locals aren't beginners though, so don't expect to get much out of the place if you're a timid rider.

The gondola runs year round, so you can get some cheap off-season flights and a proper Alpine fix without the associated costs and lengthy travel times.

## Trails

Unlike the bigger destinations which have a short summer season, the gondola at the Salève runs for most of the year and is clear of snow by mid-March. For me and likeminded bike nerds living in the northern Alpine resorts, this means gravity-assisted riding when everything else is shut – and the same goes for anyone coming from the UK. This would be great news if the trails were simply mediocre, but they're actually quite incredible, right up there with anything you'll find in the High Alps.

The main draw is the huge network of singletrack descents straight out of the lift, which have received a lot of input from local trail builders. The results are superb, with every natural gully and rocky crest utilised to full roller-coaster effect. Add to this the addictive mix of high-speed carving in the deep loam and the long drifts through the leafy forest floor and you've got a recipe for some very fun riding indeed. Things get a lot more technical as you pass below the cliff though, where only a confident rider will enjoy the loose, steep and rocky conditions leading back to the lift.

A fairly burly machine will make life easier, but make sure it's something you can pedal because there's so much more on offer if you're willing to climb a little. Heading up the ridgeline from the lift gives you access to panoramic singletracks with 360-degree views over Geneva, Annecy and Mont Blanc that can be looped back to the gondola via some steep lines through the gorge above Le Coin. Don't miss out on the Petit Salève above Monnetier either. The smooth and rolling trails here can be ridden at berserk speeds – a world away from the steep and technical riding usually associated with the Alps.

| | |
|---|---|
| ⬤—⬤ | INTERMEDIATE TO ADVANCED |
| 🏠 | 1 |
| ⬇ | 70% |
| ⬆ | 30% |
| 🕐 | 3 DAYS |
| 🧭 | TRICKY |

◄ Alpine loam just minutes from the airport – Salève.

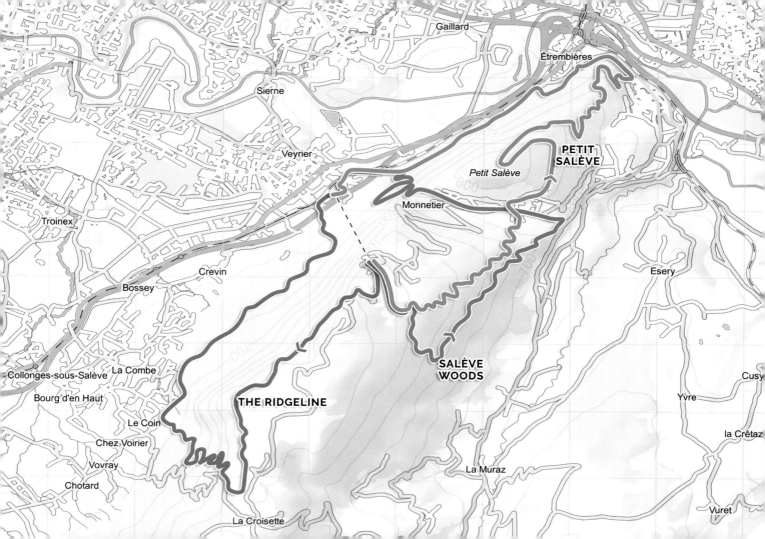

# Salève

## Our pick

### SALÈVE WOODS

The woodlands between the lift station and Monnetier are where you'll find most of the trails and other riders. None of the good stuff is marked but it's easy to find by just following your nose. The flow on these semi-natural singletracks is mind blowing, allowing you to carry speed effortlessly into the smooth jumps and drops that have been built. Every trail ends by dropping through the cliff on some steep and technical lines next to the quarry.

### THE RIDGELINE

Climb up the road from the lift and then pick up a path through the grass heading towards the cliff edge. The riding is pretty chilled as you take in the incredible vista over Geneva and the Jura mountains, but enjoy it while you can, because things get much more serious when you drop into the woods below La Croisette. The locals have worked their magic again by cutting into the steep slopes and creating some scary but very rewarding singletrack down to Le Coin. Take a trail from here all the way back to the quarry and the lift station.

## Locals' choice

### PETIT SALÈVE

Drop through the woods to Monnetier, and then look for a trail from the lower end of town that gradually winds its way up to the top of this secondary peak. From here you can charge down the ridge along some of the fastest, most balls-out trails you're ever likely to ride. The balcony trail on the north side is a more undulating affair, but beware that if you go over the edge, you'll be falling to a spectacular death on the motorway below.

## General info

A quick search on the net will bring up a few MTB videos but there's no official information on biking in the area apart from maps of the firetracks. You can find basic details about the lift and the area at: www.saleveautrement.ch

## Getting here

The Salève lift is right next to the A40 motorway, 10 minutes after passing the French border if you're coming from Geneva airport. The easiest and quickest option is a minibus transfer from the airport: www.gomassif.com

But it's also possible to catch a train and then a bus to the nearby town of Veyrier: www.tpg.ch

# Salève

## Town

The lift station is right next to the A40 motorway, taking passers by up to a viewpoint and restaurant that overlooks the lake. Apart from a public toilet which appears to be a local cottaging site, there's little else around, not even a pâtisserie and in my mind that's way more worrying than any demented pervert you might encounter. With a complete lack of cake, beer or decency in the area, this isn't a great place to stay. It works best as a day excursion from Geneva or as a stop off for anyone driving through and heading further into the mountains.

## Lift dates

The téléphérique is open all year apart from on Mondays out of season. Specific times can be seen at www.saleveautrement.ch

## Maps

The Salève IGN (*3430 OT: Mont Salève*) is the only map of the area, but even this doesn't get close to the multitude of secret trails in the woods. Some local knowledge is key – talk to other riders or give me a shout at info@bike-alp.com

## Where to stay

Camping La Colombière is 10 minutes by car from the lift in nearby Neydens: www.camping-la-colombiere.com

Staying in Geneva is another obvious option, but there's too much to go in to here. Try the usual sites like www.booking.com or www.tripadvisor.co.uk

## Eating and drinking

The posh restaurant at the top of the lift may be a little overkill for a lunchtime snack but there's a small café opposite to keep you fuelled up between runs. For a post-ride feast head to the all-you-can-eat Chinese restaurant Wowo which is just 5 minutes down the main road towards Annemasse. You'll need to go into Geneva centre to find any nightlife, with most restaurants and bars located around the old town and lakeside.

## Bike spares

Annemasse is the closest place to find any spares. Both Decathlon and Veloland both have a good range of parts as well as mechanical support if you need it.

# Samoëns and the Grand Massif

Just a short drive from Les Gets, yet still very much off the UK biking radar, Samoëns and the Grand Massif boast one of the biggest networks of lift-accessed singletrack in the Alps.

## Introduction

If you like the idea of huge descents through stunning Alpine backcountry, but would prefer to get there via ski lifts rather than days of slogging through the wilderness, then you won't find a better place in the Alps than the Grand Massif.

The main town in the system is Samoëns, about 30 minutes from Les Gets. But despite the proximity, the riding here couldn't be more dissimilar. Long, technical and steep with big freeride features where you least expect them, the trails in Samoëns are about as fun as it gets for the experienced rider, although beginners should look elsewhere.

Armed with an enduro machine, you can link up with the other resorts in the system as well, where the massive variety of trails and terrain give you a feeling of limitless possibility. The best stuff isn't easy to find, but when you do it will simply blow you away.

## Trails

The National Enduro Cup is hosted at Samoëns each year and you can see why, as the marked descents are very long and narrow in nature. These steep and technical lines have been given an injection of flow by adding catch berms and north shore jumps which are genuinely challenging to ride – perhaps too challenging for bike park fanatics making the brief hop over from Les Gets and Morzine.

Ask their opinion on the descents, and the response will often be in the form of a warning, a look of terror or even disgust in their eyes, as if they've just been abused in some way.

But really, the main draw here is the huge network of natural and untouched trails, some of which are truly epic in scale, even in Alpine terms. Because of the large height gains (the system runs from 600 to 2,500 metres), the descents can be very long and the terrain extremely varied. Riding out of the highest lift at Flaine for example, you can experience exposed shale ridgelines, endless forest switchbacks, rolling meadows and north shore features all in a single run.

These high mountain routes offer real escapism and sensational views over the Mont Blanc massif, but it's below the treeline where things get really fun. Here you'll find loamy goodness everywhere. Look a little beyond the obvious runs to find dozens of swoopy virgin trails that snake off into the woods, all of which tempt you to indulge in a glorious drift to the valley floor. The best of these are to be found off the Les Carroz gondola, and local riders will be happy to point you in the direction of the best 'brown pow'.

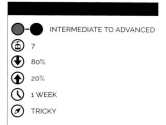

INTERMEDIATE TO ADVANCED

7

80%

20%

1 WEEK

TRICKY

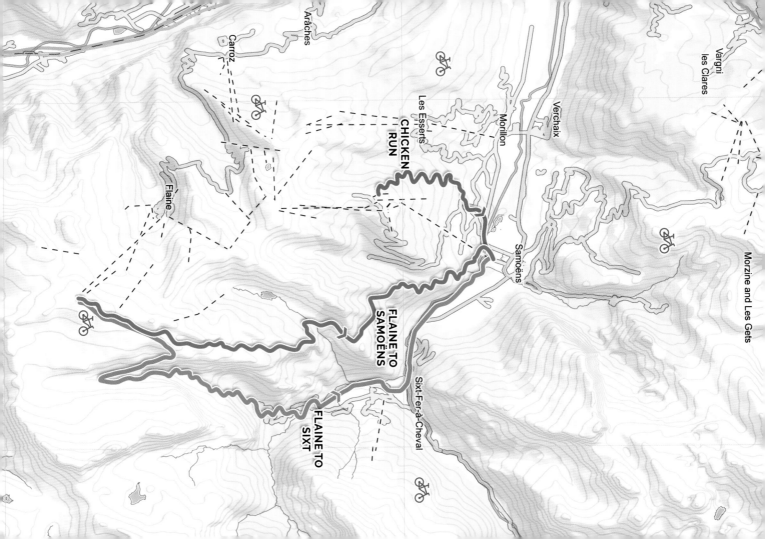

# Samoëns and the Grand Massif

## Our pick

### FLAINE TO SAMOËNS

Straight out of the Flaine gondola you'll be greeted by a spectacular panoramic vista of Mont Blanc. Head left towards Samoëns and stick to the right of the grassy peak in front of you. This is proper wilderness, and the sort of place that would normally have taken many hours of pushing to access. The fun sheep tracks winding through the shale outcrops slowly turn into a main trail which eventually brings you to the forest above Samoëns and a truly world-class singletrack with switchbacks and natural wall rides all the way into the town.

### CHICKEN RUN

A beauty built by the locals, easily spotted as a junction near the start of the black run. By taking the natural terrain and improving it as God might do if he was into mountain biking, this secret line is fast becoming legendary. Super-fast and seemingly never-ending, it sweeps through natural gullies and floats over the undulating forest floor. A silky-smooth road gap into a bermed hip jump is one of the highlights if you're feeling particularly 'on it'.

## Locals' choice

### FLAINE TO SIXT

Taking the same ridgeline as the first trail, stay high on the right-hand side to spot a ribbon of trail below, dropping into the next valley. Follow this to join up with a flat-out rocky blast, criss-crossing canyons and waterfalls all the way down to the village of Sixt and

a well-earned beer. Be aware though that this isn't an easy trail to find, so hiring a guide is well advised.

## General info

With no useful information whatsoever and impossible to navigate, the official websites of the Grand Massif will soon have you thinking 'F**k it, let's just go to Les Gets instead' – which of course is what most people end up doing. A better bet is to contact one of the local companies – try me at **www.bike-alp.com** or Jarno at **www.ridewiththelocals.com**

## Getting here

Samoëns is about an hour's drive from Geneva and around 30 minutes by car from Les Gets and Morzine via the Col de Joux Plane. Minibus transfers from the airport are available through Go Massif: **www.gomassif.com**

## Town

The idyllic town of Samoëns is now a major winter destination, but forget any ideas of typical ski resort layout or architecture. Surrounded by majestic peaks and luscious meadows, cuckoo-clock chalets make for the sort of Alpine village scene you find on chocolate box covers. Even the cows look suspiciously perfect, with bells ringing in harmonious unison. It's like a giant promotional setup for Milka itself. Despite this, a large number of bars, restaurants and general amenities mean you're well catered for during a week's stay, especially if you like cheese.

# Samoëns and the Grand Massif

## Lift dates

Opening dates vary slightly from year to year, but visiting in July and August generally guarantees open lifts. Prices here are very reasonable indeed. A week pass for the whole Grand Massif system is just 40 Euros.

For up to date information on lift dates and pricing see the Grand Massif website: tinyurl.com/grandmassif-lifts

## Maps

Trail maps don't really exist, but large displays of the routes on offer can be found at the bottom of each lift station. These cover most of the riding and you should spot plenty of other stuff along the way. The local IGN map is *3530 ET: Samoëns*.

## Where to stay

There are many hotels, chalets and apartments in Samoëns, none of which are particularly busy during the summer months. The hotels are in no way geared up for bikes so a better bet is to go for a self-catered apartment. There are plenty of options on Alps Accommodation (**www.alpsaccommodation.com**) which generally have garage space and washing facilities.

For full packages including catered accommodation, guiding and airport transfers drop me a line at **info@bike-alp.com**

## Eating and drinking

There are many restaurants in Samoëns, though not a huge variety it has to be said. Mostly the food is traditional Alpine fare – think meat and cheese.

Le 8M des Monts and Le Monde à l'Envers serve top-notch grub, but if you're looking for a big feed then head to Bar Le Savoie and La Tartinerie which offer more of a snack-based first come, first served, experience. It's basic food but lots of it.

A beer in the main square is highly recommended after a tough day's shredding, but if you really can't make it that far then Mimi's bar next to the lift is ideally situated. There is an Irish bar of course, and the jolly chaps at Covey's will make you feel more than welcome.

## Bike spares

The best option is Xtrême Glisses opposite the main lift at Samoëns. Here you'll find Kona hire bikes, disc pads, cables, mechs, tyres and disc rotors, along with armour, gloves, helmets and so forth.

# Serre Chevalier

The Serre Chevalier system is the most southern of the High Alps resorts featured here and it feels it, with a noticeably dry and arid landscape compared to the spots further north. Dusty conditions and long rear wheel drifts are guaranteed, making these gentle and swooping trails a lot of fun.

## Introduction

Despite some wonderfully designed bike park trails, a large BMX/dirt track and fantastic high-mountain enduro, this area remains completely off the radar in the summer for anyone but local riders.

Lying on the gentle and sparsely wooded slopes of the Col du Lautaret, the tracks undulate and weave through long, waterslide-style sections that invite you to get off the brakes and send it. You won't be fighting arm pump either as the loose, sandy terrain almost eliminates the build-up of braking bumps, so you can attack the descents all day long.

There's huge scope for exploring outside the marked runs as well, using the main lifts and then a little legwork to quickly get into proper Alpine wilderness.

The only things you won't find here are extreme or scary lines, the emphasis being instead on fun, flowing routes without the traffic of the bigger resorts nearby.

## Trails

The trail map indicates that Briançon is a major part of the trail network, but in fact most of this area is out of bounds to bikers. There are some decent XC loops on the other side of the valley if you fancy a bit of leg work, but really the main action takes place at the small towns of Monêtier, Villeneuve and Chantemerle further west.

At first glance this area looks fairly limited, with only a few marked trails on offer. They are only half the story though and the woods are packed with official and secret lines that make those impressive-looking parks to the north seem very average indeed. Thanks to the rolling terrain and light-density woodland, progress is intensely fast, but never very tiring due to the self-repairing nature of the sandy soil. As is often the case though, the best descents aren't on the map. Some epic lines, particularly off the Bachas lift have a real backcountry and wild appeal, and without any manicuring you'll find a few more roots and rocks on the floor. They're not intensely difficult, but you won't see anything through the clouds of dust from the guy in front, so be sure to pack an extra tube and mech hanger!

This sandy terrain in the woods gives a coastal Mediterranean feel to the riding, but there is opportunity for some proper backcountry stuff too, particularly if you head south from the Serre Chevalier peak and then loop behind the Eychauda summit to meet up with the Monêtier trails. You're never too far away from the park, but as you set off towards the wilderness of the Écrins and its huge summits and glaciers, this really does feel like big mountain exploration.

 INTERMEDIATE TO ADVANCED

 3

 80%

 20%

 1 WEEK

 NOT TOO BAD

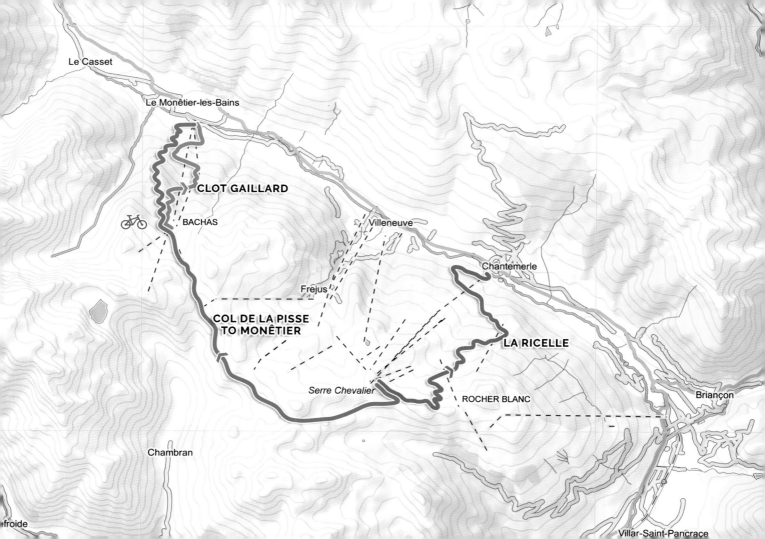

# Serre Chevalier

## Our pick
### LA RICELLE
From the Serre Chevalier peak, head east down this stunning ridgeline to the Rocher Blanc. A singletrack dropping back into the valley to the left will have you jumping out of your skin with excitement. It doesn't disappoint either, effortlessly flowing through the gorse-lined terrain before launching you into the pines below and back to Chantemerle. Long, fast and very fun without too much to worry about, it's a great intro and typical of the riding here.

### COL DE LA PISSE TO MONÊTIER
A big enduro loop from the Ratier lift. Dropping east down the ridge, take a right and drop back underneath the Serre Chevalier peak to traverse to the Col de la Pisse. With a backdrop of huge scree fields and jagged peaks, this high-mountain route is simply stunning. The trail gradually descends to the Bachas lift station. From here head left behind the ridgeline to pick up a magical singletrack through a forgotten valley. Technical and seemingly endless, you'll roll into Monêtier with a massive grin (and possibly cow shit) on your face.

## Locals' choice
### CLOT GAILLARD
The chaps at Monêtier sure know how to build a trail. Taking an existing path and building berms in all the right places, this red run will definitely have you coming back for more. As you charge over the crests and natural rollers, a wonderful sensation of being weightless means you simply cannot bear to hit the brakes and make it stop. The swoopy lower section through the terraced fields is pure joy too.

## General info
The area has a dedicated bike park site, with good maps and info on the trails as well as a couple of videos: www.bikepark-serrechevalier.com

The tourist info site has a bit more info on the wider area: tinyurl.com/serrechevalier-info

## Getting here
The nearest airports are Grenoble (around 3.5 hours) and Turin (3 hours). Briançon sits at the bottom of the Col du Lautaret and the Col de Montgenèvre. So although it's not the easiest area to access, it's a beautiful drive from either direction. Briançon is on the French main lines so it's not too painful to get here by train: www.voyages-sncf.com

# Serre Chevalier

## Town

Villeneuve is the best of the small towns that make up the system, with a good selection of bars and restaurants to choose from. Another option is the large regional centre of Briançon just 15 minutes away. This offers a little more in the way of culture, having been heavily fortified in the past to defend the region against the Austrians and their liberal approach to mountain biking. Now a world heritage site, the city adds a different element to a biking trip with none of that 'dead ski resort' feel that typifies many other Alpine destinations.

## Lift dates

From early July to early September: **tinyurl.com/serrechevalier-lifts**

## Maps

Maps are available at the various lift stations or online here: **tinyurl.com/serrechevalier-maps**. For more detail, you want IGN *3536 OT: Briançon*.

## Where to stay

It's best to stay in Villeneuve or Briançon as they're where most of the action is. With most ski accommodation empty during the summer it's not hard to find a place to stay. Many options can be found on the tourist info site: **tinyurl.com/serrechevalier-accommodation**

Another good option is **www.apartmentbriancon.com** which has a number of apartments in the centre of Briançon.

## Eating and drinking

During the day it's best to head to Villeneuve where most trails meet up. A good option here is Le Frog bar near the main lift, which serves decent burgers and even fish and chips for the committed Brit abroad. La Grotte bar is a local favourite and often has live music in the evening. Back in Briançon there's really no need to go anywhere but the Pâtisserie Turin which is a big shop full of cakes. With its large outdoor terrace, Le Club 25 in the centre is another popular local hang-out.

## Bike spares

Phillipe Sports and SportRent just below the Caisse du Boeuf lift have some basic spares, Commençal hire bikes and local guides.

# Tignes and Val d'Isère (Espace Killy)

Located high up amongst the rocky peaks and glaciers of the Tarentaise valley, this giant bike park boasts a huge number of trails for all abilities. Forget any notions of forest singletrack and exploring forgotten valleys – this no-nonsense park is all about big berms, big bikes and big views.

## Introduction

Most ski resorts simply shut down once the winter has passed, but no one could accuse Tignes of being non-proactive during the summer months. A huge amount of investment has been put into the bike park – the stark and rocky landscape scarred with dozens of trails that cater to all abilities. The Superenduro and DH world cup in Val d'Isère has also cemented the area as a serious biking destination, and as if this weren't enough, the whole thing is totally free to use throughout the season! With most of the riding being above 2,000 metres, a big mountain experience with stunning views is guaranteed, as are fast-draining, all-weather trails.

The lack of any woodland and only a handful of man-made enduro lines means you'll spend most of your time on wide-open descents, so a downhill-specific machine is the bike of choice here.

## Trails

Only the Portes du Soleil can rival the amount of time and investment that this area has put into its purpose-built trails. Tignes in particular likes to compare itself with Les Gets and Morzine, claiming bigger and better runs, fewer braking bumps and smaller lift queues.

Much of that might be true, but there is one major drawback here that doesn't affect the PdS. The Espace Killy is located in the Vanoise national park, where mountain biking is banned. Therefore you're limited to the marked routes, with little scope for exploring or riding natural trails without a lot of opposition and the threat of fines.

To make up for this, the trail builders have attempted to create some technical enduro routes by hand. It's a good effort, but they just don't give the same satisfaction as proper natural trails. The real draw here is in the fast and open DH tracks that brilliantly utilise the rocky landscape. Despite the high altitude, the terrain is surprisingly mellow on the Val d'Isère side, with long winding reds off the Solaise and Olympique lifts proving a lot of fun on a big bike. Heading over to Tignes, things start to get a little more serious down the black runs of the Tovière and downright ridiculous on the 'double black elite' runs with their massive jumps. The big smooth rock faces that feature on this side of the mountain are also integrated into the trail, with some ingenious sections such as the 360-degree wall ride.

With a huge network of descents and nothing too unexpected on the trails to catch you out, this is a great place for those wanting to smash out a day's descending with minimal pedal time. Anyone looking to get away from it all or seek out swoopy woodland singletrack should look elsewhere though.

|  |  |
|---|---|
| ●-● | BEGINNER TO ADVANCED |
| 🎫 | 5 |
| ⬇ | 90% |
| ⬆ | 10% |
| 🕐 | 1 WEEK |
| 🧭 | EASY |

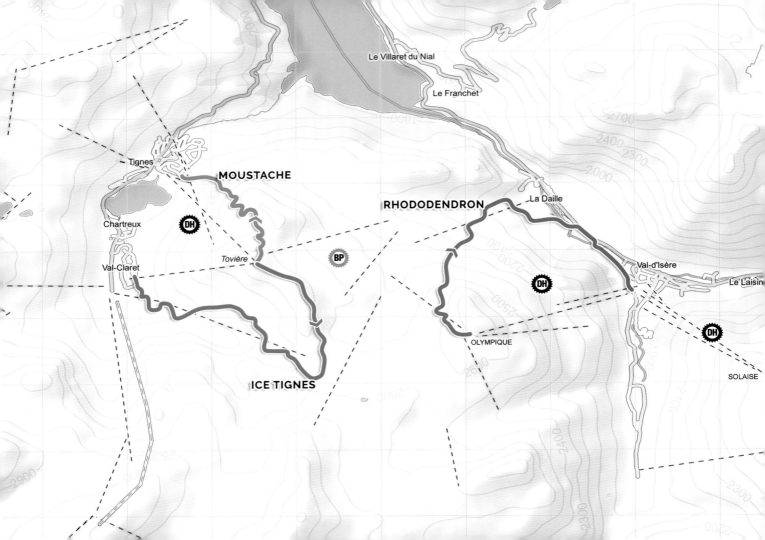

Le Villaret du Nial

Le Franchet

Tignes

**MOUSTACHE**

Chartreux

**RHODODENDRON**

La Daille

DH

Val-Claret

Tovière

BP

Val-d'Isère

Le Laisin

DH

**ICE TIGNES**

OLYMPIQUE

DH

SOLAISE

# Tignes and Val d'Isère (Espace Killy)

## Our pick

### ICE TIGNES

Big thrills are to be had along this knife-edge ridgeline, which is the closest thing you'll get to a natural trail in Tignes. From Tovière you'll see the path heading up the ridge in front of you. With 360-degree views over the glaciers and with massive drops on either side, this singletrack picks its way around the rocky outcrops. It takes some balls to ride the really exposed sections, but it flows very well if you can stomach it. High Alpine giddiness guaranteed.

### MOUSTACHE

This black run above the Lac de Tignes makes brilliant use of natural features, rolling up over huge boulders and threading through tight gullies. Steep and sometimes quite intense, it makes the lower *Gypsy* trail seem very easy going. A great mix-up that utilises the best of the Tignes terrain.

## Locals' choice

### RHODODENDRON

You can let the brakes off and really let the bike run along this flowing red run that winds around the Bellevarde peak into Val d'Isère. Smooth, mid-sized drops and jumps give a wonderful floating feel to this long descent. The lower section offers one of the few wooded sections on the mountain as well, adding a bit of variety to the riding.

## General info

There's a lot of information on the net. The official site is refreshingly informative: **tinyurl.com/tignes-bikepark**

Local man Nick Gowan has also produced a great site with videos, news and photos on the park: **startlinemtb.com**

## Getting here

Val d'Isère and Tignes sit on the Col de l'Iseran, around 2 hours from Chambéry by car. Cool Bus runs transfers from Chambéry, Grenoble and Geneva: **www.thecoolbus.co.uk**

# Tignes and Val d'Isère (Espace Killy)

## Town

Situated high on the Col de l'Iseran, the Espace Killy is one of the highest resorts in the Alps, with summer skiing available on the glacier at Tignes. The snowy peaks provide some beautiful surroundings for biking, which is a good thing because the drab sixties look of Tignes makes for a grim venue indeed. Neither Tignes nor Val d'Isère are particularly lively during the summer months either, so they're not the greatest of places to stay. A few bars and restaurants remain open though, so there's enough to keep you alive for a week.

## Lift dates

From the last weekend in June to the end of August. Dates are posted in the spring at **tinyurl.com/tignes-info**

## Maps

A map can be obtained from the lift office in Tignes or Val d'Isère, or online at **tinyurl.com/tignes-info**. As bikes are banned outside the park you're unlikely to need anything more than this.

## Where to stay

There are many options in either town, with many ski apartments and hotels empty for the summer. Startline MTB can source most options for you: **startlinemtb.com**

For accommodation in Val have a look at their official page here: **tinyurl.com/valdisere-accommodation**

## Eating and drinking

Both towns really wind down after the winter so you won't find any raucous activity on offer. However there's enough to keep you going with most of the action in Tignes-le-Lac. Good options are the Loop Bar for a burger and a beer and Le Coin des Amis in Val which is popular with the locals. It's never a sure thing which restaurants will be open each summer so just see what you can find!

## Bike spares

The Intersports in Val and Tignes have Scott hire bikes and some very basic spares. Startline MTB in Tignes-Le-Lac has Specialized and Mondraker bikes to rent as well as a few spares: **startlinemtb.com**

◄ You can't ride outside the park in Tignes, but it never seems to matter.

# Valloire

With some big-name neighbours taking all the limelight, Valloire doesn't get the attention it deserves. In terms of quality rather than quantity, the beautiful and untouched trails here beat the big boys hands down – a little exploring opens up some truly spectacular Alpine singletracks to rival anything, anywhere.

## Introduction

Valloire sits in between the Col du Galibier and the Col du Télégraphe – a hot spot throughout the summer for masochists with a lycra fetish. But rather than concentrating all their efforts on road riding, the town has done a superb job on the mountain bike front. It's largely unheard of though, for a couple of reasons. Firstly, those in the biking community really want to keep this gem to themselves. Secondly, if you're researching the riding in the area, you'll undoubtedly be drawn to some of the biggest names in the business – nearby Deux Alpes and Alpe d'Huez are in the next valleys, are easier to access and market their biking with sledgehammer subtlety. That's OK though, because the low numbers and spectacular surroundings mean that the Valloire trails are pretty special indeed, and well worth the effort to visit.

## Trails

The trail map leaves you quite uninspired, but don't let it fool you – the bike park contains some wonderful natural-feeling trails with a helping hand given here and there just to help the flow. The hardpack descents don't receive the traffic associated with the big resorts, so they're smooth and fast as a result. That's not to say that riding here is a walk in the park, as many of the trails feature roots, rocks and some hairy north shore contraptions, so beginners may be a little overwhelmed.

The marked runs under the main lift are great, but head higher up on the Lac de la Vieille lift and you'll find ridgeline singletrack blasts designed so well that you wonder why on earth you haven't heard more of this place. One imagines a large network of riders are continuously working on the routes here, but the staff will tell you it's all built by one man. ONE MAN! Resorts with diggers and designated teams of trail builders can't do anything nearly as good. I want to find this bloke and shake him frantically, demanding to know how he could possibly have done this.

However, even this genius can't beat the work of Mother Nature. Head into the combe towards the Aiguille Noire and you'll be greeted by ribbons of picture-perfect singletrack that wind down through the meadows and disappear into the stunning scenery beyond. It's also possible to drop over the ridge into the Valmeinier side before traversing back to the Col du Télégraphe and back to Valloire. Exploring is fairly safe and easy to do here as you're only using the one ridgeline, so don't be afraid to experiment as there's a whole lot more than you'll see on the modest trail map.

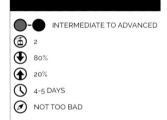

⬤-⬤  INTERMEDIATE TO ADVANCED

2

80%

20%

4-5 DAYS

NOT TOO BAD

◀ The work of a trail-building genius – the *Sapinière* trail.

VALLOIRE    **205**

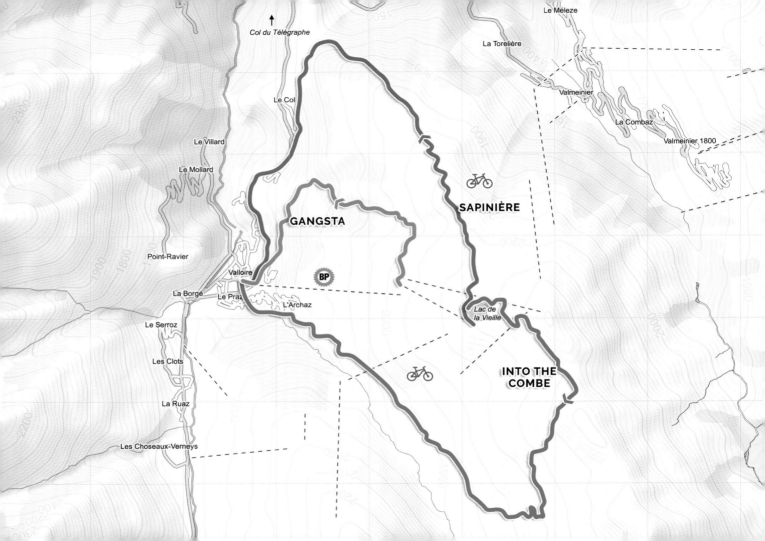

Col du Télégraphe

Le Mélèze

La Torelière

Le Col

Valmeinier

Le Villard

La Combaz

Le Mollard

Valmeinier 1800

**GANGSTA**

**SAPINIÈRE**

Point-Ravier

Valloire

**BP**

La Borgé

Le Praz

L'Archaz

Lac de
la Vieille

Le Serroz

Les Clots

**INTO THE
COMBE**

La Ruaz

Les Choseaux-Verneys

# Valloire

## Our pick

### INTO THE COMBE

I can tell you now that the high Alpine singletrack that occupies your dreams actually exists. From the top lift, climb up above the Lac de la Vieille and bear to the right, riding up onto the ridgeline. As the trail turns into a narrow path you'll find a turn off on the right. This is just about perfect as it winds down into the gorge, the huge rock faces behind adding an epic backdrop. Follow your nose back into Valloire along anything that looks good – you can't really go wrong!

### SAPINIÈRE

This red route off the top lift is a corker. Take a left and head straight down the ridge. There's nothing particularly demanding about the trail, which is a let-the-brakes-off-and-go-for-it affair, but you can let the brakes off for about eleven kilometres, making it pretty unique. A must if you're lucky enough to ride here.

## Locals' choice

### GANGSTA

The local chaps seem pretty taken with the run named *Gangsta*. Heading left out of the first lift, follow the blue until you see the turn off. As it drops into the trees it really picks up speed, rolling through the gentle terrain with roller-coaster-style features. A favourite amongst gangsters apparently.

## General info

For all things Valloire the official website is actually pretty good: tinyurl.com/valloire-info

## Getting here

Valloire can be accessed either from the Oisans side via the Col du Galibier, about 1.5 hours from Les Deux Alpes. Or if you're travelling down from the north it's a fairly easy drive from Albertville, following signs for the Col du Télégraphe.

# Valloire

## Town

Valloire sits in beautiful surroundings, with the Galibier peaks providing some majestic backdrops. The town itself has a wonderfully chilled atmosphere, but they're really quite 'on it' in terms of the biking – the lifts are fast and continuous (no 30-minute waits between gondolas here) with a good set-up for bikes. There are plenty of reasonably priced accommodation options, restaurants and a couple of bars too, so although it's not a riot in the evenings, it's not totally dead either, with more than enough entertainment for a few nights.

## Lift dates

As with most French resorts, July and August are the only safe bets. Specific dates can be found on www.valloire.net

## Maps

Bike and hiking trail maps are available from the tourist info in the town centre and at the ticket office at the lift. The local IGN map is *3435 ET: Valloire*.

## Where to stay

Situated opposite the main lift, the Patchwork Altitude hotel is ideal, offering secure bike storage, a workshop and the use of the pool. A room with breakfast and dinner can be had for under 60 Euros a night. Although note that at the time of publication (2015) the hotel is closed for renovations. www.patchworkaltitude.com

## Eating and drinking

Most popular is the Hôtel du Centre, which is busy most evenings. Also worth checking out is the Mast'Rock which often has live music.

Pizzerias are the name of the game here and can be found everywhere. The pizzeria next to the lift is pretty good but if you're looking for even greater amounts of cheese, head for La Grange de Thelcide, which serves up Savoyard fare such as fondues and crêpes.

## Bike spares

For some very basic spares head to Magnin Sports, which also hires out Lapierre machines, or Ski Set, which rents out Commençal bikes.

◄ 'A little exploring opens up some truly spectacular Alpine singletracks to rival anything, anywhere.'

VALLOIRE  **209**

# Verbier

Sitting high on the sunny slopes of the Valais, Verbier boasts a mouth-watering array of world-class singletracks that remain in great condition despite the increasing number of trail riders that flock here every summer. The park is top quality too, so there's plenty of variety to keep things interesting.

## Introduction

The scope for natural riding in the Valais is simply incredible, but Verbier is one of the few resorts to really tap into it in any commercial way. It's worked too, and thousands now come here from the world over to ride classic Swiss singletrack with the benefits of lift access. The trails may not be as untouched as some of the best in the area, but they still retain a real backcountry feel and can be extremely challenging to ride due to the steep gradients, tight switchbacks and epic lengths.

You're not confined to the immediate bowl either, with the option of dropping into La Tzoumaz over the northern ridge and then hooking up with other lift systems along the Sion valley such as Nendaz and Veysonnaz to ride some huge enduro loops. Many companies now exist in Verbier and the lower Châble valley and they can help you explore the best of the surrounding region, using uplifts to extend the riding area even further.

## Trails

The majority of the marked trails run between the Ruinettes lift and Verbier town at 1,500 metres. This *only* gives around 700 metres of vertical drop and there aren't a huge number of runs, but none of that matters when the descents are this well designed. In fact, this is one of the best spots I've ridden, with lines that not only flow, but feature roots, rocky step ups and tight switchbacks that reward the technical rider.

The only real downside to this is that there isn't a huge amount for beginners, who will quickly become either awesome or dead if they try and tackle anything other than the double track which swings out to either side of the Verbier bowl.

These contouring firetracks aren't great in themselves, but they're ideal for gaining access to Verbier's party piece, which is the wealth of big mountain singletrack on offer. From the Ruinettes lift you can cruise out either side to pick up a number of beautiful snaking lines that twist and turn all the way down to the valley floor almost 1,500 vertical metres below. You can then take the Châble lift from Villette back up to Verbier and do it all over again.

Most of these trails are easy to spot but they're far from easy to ride, with rock gardens, tight switchbacks and exposed root sections being regular features. If you're a good rider though, it really doesn't get any better than these relentless descents that will have you screaming with arm pump and whooping with joy all at the same time.

The scope for big enduro loops doesn't stop here, as you can easily drop into La Tzoumaz from the Savoleyres lift and then attempt some epic circuits via Nendaz and the marked 'Tour du Mont-Fort'. Hook up with a local guiding company here and the limits are pushed even further, so there's enough natural riding to keep the purist happy for a long, long time.

## ENDURO/DOWNHILL

 INTERMEDIATE TO ADVANCED

 4

 80%

 20%

🕐 1 WEEK

🧭 NOT TOO BAD

◄ Verbier awesomeness – La Chaux to Le Morgnes.

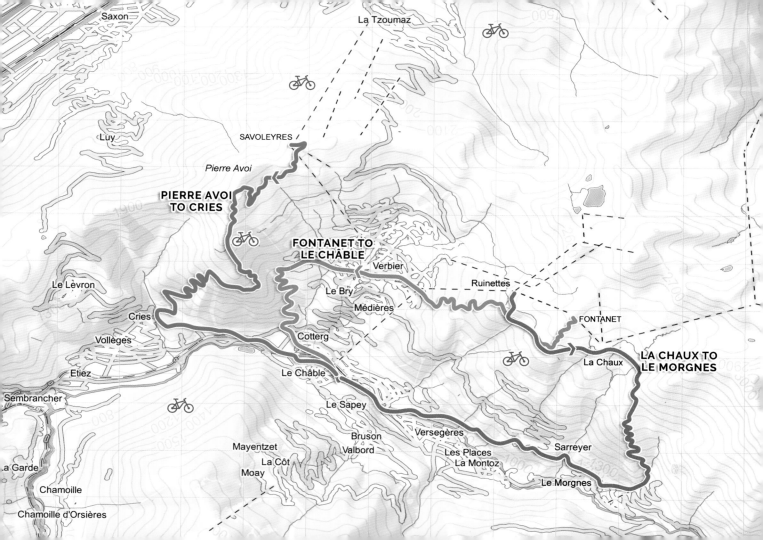

# Verbier

## Our pick
### PIERRE AVOI TO CRIES

From the Savoleyres lift drop down to the west and meet up with the main double track that swings around the bowl. Follow this until the track stops, get your bike on your back and hike up the small trail to your right which brings you out just below the Pierre Avoi peak. It's a bit of a slog but definitely worth it when you see the mouth-watering singletrack that winds off towards the stunning backdrop of Mont Blanc and the Grand Combin. As you head into the woods look for the signs to Vollèges which bring you on to a loamy trail known locally as *Jackass*. This is steep terrain and some of the corners cannot be ridden, but the good bits are very good indeed, getting faster and faster as you drop down. Finish in the aptly named village of Cries, which is exactly what you'll be doing when you finally pry your hands from the bars. From here just roll down the double track to your left and back to the Châble lift.

### FONTANET TO LE CHÂBLE

A huge adrenaline-hit of park and nature with over 1,500 metres of vertical height loss. Head up to the top of the Fontanet lift, where you can roll straight into the new *Rodze* red run which packs dozens of mid-sized jumps into its modest length and links straight into the *Wouaiy* run (which presumably should be pronounced in a lairy British builder fashion). This is a great trail, mixing smooth and flowing jump lines with tight, sandy switchbacks and rooty drop-offs. Keep the adrenaline flowing by dropping into the small black section at the bottom, which is a heady mix of pure trials through the rock gardens and tricky freeride obstacles. Most will choose to finish in Verbier, but if you head to the far western side of town (to St Christophe) you'll spot a singletrack dropping off the road to the left which charges all the way down to the Châble lift on the valley floor.

## Locals' choice
### LA CHAUX TO LE MORGNES

From the top of the Ruinettes lift head east and climb along the double track, following signs to La Chaux. As you turn around the spine you'll spot a rocky track below the ridgeline in front of you. This leads you to the start of a sublime trail that follows the spine all the way to the valley floor. Unlike many of the natural lines here, the tight switchbacks are often set deep in natural gullies which mean you can properly rail them and keep on the gas. Big grins are guaranteed by the time you finally reach Le Morgnes, where you can either climb up to Sarreyer and get a bit more trail time, or just roll down the road back to Le Châble and let those warped discs cool down a little.

# Verbier

## General info

Verbier has a dedicated site to the park with information on dates and prices as well as photos, videos and trail maps: **www.verbierbikepark.ch**

Also check out Verbinet for some ideas on accommodation and a general overview of the area: **www.verbinet.com**

## Getting here

The resort of Verbier sits high on the sunny slopes above the Bagnes valley, just 30 minutes from Martigny by car and not far from Chamonix (1.5 hours) if you fancy a bit of nightlife one evening.

If you're driving down from the UK then the quickest route is to head to Geneva and then follow the lake on either side before turning south towards Martigny. Airport transfers can be booked through AlpineXpress: **www.alpinexpress.com**

It's also possible to catch a train from Geneva to Le Châble and then take a bus or the lift up to Verbier: **www.sbb.ch**

## Town

The famous ski resort of Verbier isn't quite as lively in summer as in winter, but there's still enough to keep you entertained when the lifts stop running, with a few high-priced bars and restaurants happily draining you of cash in typical Swiss style. Accommodation is pricey compared to the French resorts, but the summer prices will seem like an absolute bargain compared to mid-winter tariffs. There are many other riders staying in the town though, so there's a familiar and likeminded vibe which makes for a great place to chill with a post-ride beer and watch the late evening sun drop behind Mont Blanc.

## Lift dates

Like all Swiss resorts Verbier boasts a long season compared to its French and Italian neighbours, with lifts running from June through to late October. Specific times and prices can be found here: **www.verbierbikepark.ch**

## Maps

A map of the park, enduro and XC routes can be obtained at the Châble and Ruinettes lift stations. Alternatively you can download it online from **www.verbierbikepark.ch**. Swiss National Map *1325: Sembrancher* covers the immediate area, but you'll need *1326: Rosablanche* if you start heading east.

◄ The switchback – a staple of Alpine riding. At least this one isn't rocky.

# Verbier

## Where to stay

For many, staying with a bike-specific company is the best option here as they'll have you riding all the secret bits as well as offering a stress-free package. The most well-established are Bike Verbier and MTB Verbier: **www.bikeverbier.com** and **www.mtbverbier.com**

If you fancy doing your own thing then the official site has a list of bike-friendly hotels which offer facilities such as a bike wash and secure storage: **tinyurl.com/verbier-accommodation**.

If you're just visiting for a day or two with your own transport then consider stopping at the lift at Le Châble. There's a huge parking area here and it means you avoid the drive up to Verbier.

## Eating and drinking

Located close to the Ruinettes lift, the Pub Mont Fort is one of the original Verbier bars and is still hugely popular, with a good range of beers, cocktails and live music or DJs in the evenings. Tasty burgers and international dishes make it good spot for a feed too. A more chilled venue can be found at the Farinet bar on the main street, where you can slump in sofas next to the fire and lazily pick at the day's scabs. Afterwards head to the Farm Club for some seedy late-night antics.

## Bike spares

There are a few ski-rental-turned-bike-shops throughout the town centre. One of the best is Jet Verbier, which has Scott bikes for hire as well as a decent selection of spares.

◄ Railing the Pierre Avoi.

# Zermatt

One of the most iconic peaks in the business, the Matterhorn stands guard over some breathtaking singletrack that never seems to end. Those views cost serious money though, making Zermatt prohibitively expensive for all but the most committed or affluent of riders.

## Introduction

Famous the world over for that pointy rock at the end of the valley, Switzerland's premier resort needs little introduction. Hikers, climbers and skiers flock here throughout the year, laying down some serious cash to get a glimpse of the Matterhorn. Is it worth it? Well personally I hate hiking and cannot see the point of skiing in the summer, and there are plenty of other 'cheaper' mountains in the Alps that are every bit as stunning. However, there's no denying that this a very special place to ride indeed, with magical trails that take you on a full-throttle Alpine adventure through the dazzling glacial peaks to the wooded valleys below.

Don't expect a smooth and easy ride though. It may be flowing for the most part, but this is proper high-altitude stuff where you'll encounter exposed and very technical riding, so beginner or intermediate riders looking to tick one off the list will come away frustrated.

## Trails

It's hard to find fault with the quality and scope of riding on offer in Zermatt. Even those looking for some park riding can session the DH and 4-Cross tracks from the Sunnegga funicular, but this really is missing the point. You're far better off continuing up the lift to the Rothorn where the true spirit of Zermatt riding stretches out before you in snaking, flowing, singletrack form. The route from here that cuts across the face of the Oberrothorn is simply incredible, but save it for the end of the day as the full descent drops you right back down into Täsch, where you will have left the car (see 'The Town').

In the meantime, take your pick from the epic lines from the Gornergrat train and Schwarzsee lift under the Matterhorn. The Gornergrat is the most popular for riders and walkers alike and it's easy to see why, with an impressive panorama over the Monte Rosa, Riffelsee and Matterhorn. Try not to be too put off by the hordes of tourists staggering down the trails and staring at the backs of their iPads, as they tend not to get too far and you'll soon have the mountain to yourself.

Then you can let rip, either straight down the ridge towards the Riffelhorn or cutting back across the mountain and heading for the Sunnegga spine. Either direction takes you on a roller-coaster ride across the rocky landscape, covering everything from steep and technical sections to gentle flowing lines where you can get off the brakes and send it. Eventually you end up in the Riffelalp or Sunnegga forests, which although still rocky and hard-packed rather than loamy, add some great variety to the descents, as well as offering many routes back into the town.

More singletrack heaven can be found quite easily from the Schwarzsee lift, but if you really want to experience the whole area, consider getting away from it all with a local guide who'll show you some great stuff further down the valley at St Niklaus and Stalden.

| SINGLETRACK/ENDURO | |
|---|---|
| ⬤ | ADVANCED |
| 🎫 | 5 |
| ⬇ | 80% |
| ⬆ | 20% |
| 🕐 | 4–5 DAYS |
| 🧭 | NOT TOO BAD |

◀ The ever-distracting backdrop of the Matterhorn.

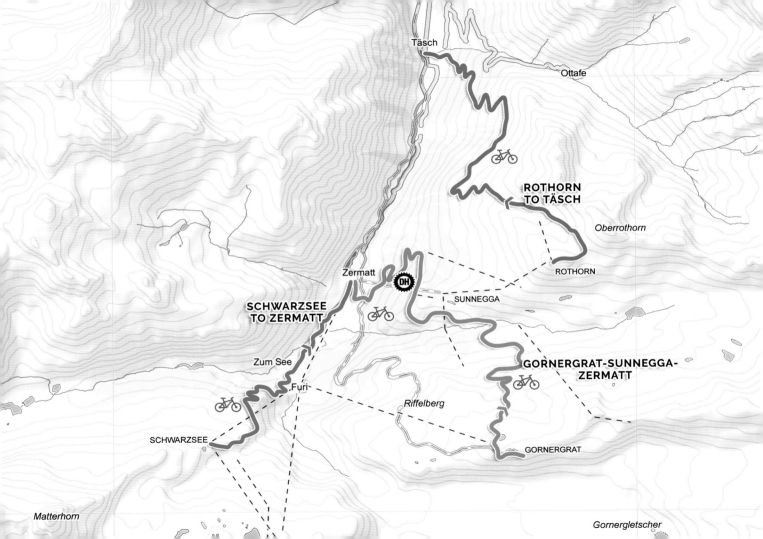

Täsch

Ottafe

**ROTHORN
TO TÄSCH**

*Oberrothorn*

ROTHORN

Zermatt

DH

SUNNEGGA

**SCHWARZSEE
TO ZERMATT**

**GORNERGRAT-SUNNEGGA-
ZERMATT**

Zum See

Furi

*Riffelberg*

SCHWARZSEE

GORNERGRAT

*Matterhorn*

*Gornergletscher*

# Zermatt

## Our pick

### ROTHORN TO TÄSCH

If you only ride one descent in Zermatt (or anywhere for that matter), make it this swoopy singletrack charge from the Rothorn to Täsch, over 1,500 metres below on the valley floor. Ride straight out of the back of the lift to pick up a track cutting across the huge scree slope of the Oberrothorn. Words can't really describe how good this is; suffice to say you'll never want to ride a park trail again. Picking up another singletrack coming from the Sunnegga, you can then traverse across the mountain following signs for Täschalp, before plunging into the forest and keeping an eye out for the cheeky lines that cut across the firetrack and deliver you to Täsch.

### GORNERGRAT–SUNNEGGA–ZERMATT

Resist the urge to follow everyone else down the ridge and instead take a right just below the top station, through a small tunnel underneath the train lines. Head towards the lake below where you'll pick up a trail signed for the Grünsee lake and the Sunnegga. This gently descending line is great fun, but it gets even better as you drop into the woods below the lake and then on to the Sunnegga ridge. As you pass by the Mosjesee lake follow the signs for the village of Ze Gassen. Just below this, take a right and traverse through the forest to find a smooth and flowing singletrack that dips in and out of the trees to reveal some magnificent views of the Matterhorn in the distance. Follow the signs to Zermatt and the last section reveals a bit of root and loam that you can shred back into the town.

### SCHWARZSEE TO ZERMATT

Take a left out of the Schwarzsee lift and head down the ridge to pick up a glorious switchback-filled run that cuts back under the lift before dropping through the woods into Furi. This is one of those trails that just keeps getting faster and more fun as you go down, with the steep and rocky terrain up top slowly turning into a silent and floaty charge through the deep pine needles of the forest below. From Furi simply follow the signs back into Zermatt.

# Zermatt

## General info

Like most of the Swiss resorts, Zermatt is really quite 'on it' in terms of marketing and tourism. The official site is a great place to start and tells you everything you need to know about the area, as well having a dedicated section on biking with route ideas: **www.zermatt.ch/en**

## Getting here

Zermatt sits close to the Swiss/Italian border in the southern Valais region of Switzerland. The airports of Bern, Zurich and Geneva all offer train connections to the resort at around 3 to 3.5 hours' transfer time: **www.sbb.ch**

If you're driving from the UK you're looking at a 3-hour drive from Geneva to Täsch via Montreux and Martigny, where you can then catch a train up to Zermatt.

If you're feeling flush you can hire a private taxi with Alphubel Taxi who can take you direct from the airports up to Zermatt ... for a price: **www.zermatt-airport-transfers.com**

## Town

The car-free resort of Zermatt requires you to leave your vehicle down the valley at Täsch and then take a train into the town itself. As a result, most riders can be found down near Täsch in the evenings, staying at the various campsites and parking areas near the station. It's worth heading into Zermatt for some post-ride entertainment though, as the centre is a buzzing summer venue with many bars and restaurants on offer where live music and late-night antics are a regular occurrence. Try to imagine a Swiss version of Chamonix and you'll get the idea: a famous mountain, great riding and lots of nightlife – as well as thousands of tourists. Just minus the traffic jams.

## Lift dates

Zermatt has a long summer season, with most lifts running from May until mid-October. Be aware though that because of the high altitude you may find a lot of snow on the trails before mid-June. Lift passes are split between the Gornergrat train or the Sunnegga and Schwarzsee areas. This does allow you to pick and choose which runs you do but even then the prices are sickening. A day's pass on the Gornergrat alone is pushing 80 Euros, so a week's riding could get very expensive indeed. All the prices are listed on the official site: **tinyurl.com/zermatt-biking**

◄ Utterly beautiful. You can't beat Zermatt for scenery – Gornergrat.

# Zermatt

## Maps

The official site (**tinyurl.com/zermatt-biking**) has some route ideas as well as maps that can be downloaded on to a phone or Google Earth, although many of the itineraries ignore the lifts and make for a sadistic slog of pain from the valley floor. A better option is the Biking Spots site which lists some of the best descents on offer as well as plotting each route on OS/IGN-style maps: **www.bikingspots.ch**. Swiss National Map *1348: Zermatt* covers the town itself and the Gornergrat train, but you'll need *1328: Randa* if you're heading down the valley towards Täsch.

## Where to stay

You aren't allowed to drive up to Zermatt itself, so anyone driving here will have to leave the car at nearby Täsch, just down the valley. Here you'll find many camping spots as well as restaurants and hotels that have sprung up to cater for those looking to ease the financial strain of visiting Zermatt. One of the best is Camping Täsch, which is located next to the river and close to the train station for Zermatt: **www.campingtaesch.ch**

If you would rather be a little closer to the action then have a look at the tourist info site which lists a range of hotels in Zermatt that feature bike-friendly facilities such as washing areas and secure storage: **tinyurl.com/zermatt-accommodation**

It's also worth considering a bike-specific chalet, not only because a week in Zermatt is a very costly option, but because you'll get to ride a few of the great riding areas nearby such as Saas-Fee, Crans-Montana and the Anniviers valley. OTP is one the most popular local operators: **www.otp.co.uk**

## Eating and drinking

Zermatt has one of the best and largest selections of nightlife you're likely to experience in a summer Alpine resort. You do pay for it of course, but there are some reasonable options, such as the large and tasty burgers at Brown Cow Pub washed down with some local cider. One of the great things about Zermatt is the variety on offer and there aren't many biking venues that offer live piano bars as post-ride entertainment – like GramPi's pub with its love of eighties classics. Other popular drinking spots include the Papperla Pub and Elsie's Bar.

## Bike spares

The Mountain Shack in the centre of town has Nukeproof hire bikes and a few spares in stock: **www.themountainshack.com**

Into the wilds above Annecy.

# More riding – Aravis
# (near Megève, La Clusaz and Les Saisies)

## Annecy

The beautiful lakeside city of Annecy is well worth a visit, especially if you're in La Clusaz, which is only 30 or 40 minutes away by car. The crystal-clear waters and medieval town justify the short drive down here by themselves, but what most people don't know is just how good the riding is in the surrounding hills. Untouched and impossibly picturesque trails can be found all around the lake, but the best stuff is on the Semnoz – a long ridgeline to the west of the lake.

During July and August you can catch a bus from opposite the mairie to the top of the Semnoz and the main trailhead. Outside these times it's possible to climb the long but gently inclined road to the top in around 1.5 hours. It's a long slog, but the huge descent which finishes back in the town is an absolute corker. It's rocky, technical, rooty and very fast all at the same time, with mini climbs that keep the heart rate up and the descent going for almost an hour – Alpine enduro in its purest form. Just be sure to avoid the marked bike trail, which is little more than a narrow road. French IGN map *3431 OT: Lac d'Annecy* will help you find the trails.

Geneva is the nearest airport to Annecy, although it's a fairly easy run up the motorway from Grenoble. It's also not too far to drive here from many of the major areas in this book, with good roads from the Chamonix and Bourg-Saint-Maurice regions making Annecy a potential stop on a car journey to or from the UK. Accommodation-wise, there are numerous choices in Annecy itself, or any number of campsites down the sides of the lake.

Lose the crowds in Beaufortain.

# More riding – Aravis
## (near Megève, La Clusaz and Les Saisies)

## Beaufortain

Megéve and Les Saisies lie on the edge of an area commonly referred to as 'Spot X', otherwise known as the Beaufortain region. This huge area just west of the Mont Blanc range receives very few visitors in the summer, so that feeling of isolation and adventure is easy to achieve. The huge enduro routes from Les Saisies into Albertville on page 107 typify the type of riding on offer here (think moist and rooty rather than dry and rocky), but it's only the tip of the iceberg, as many bike-specific tour companies are finding out.

Using the local bus links that run from the lower valleys (see Les Saisies, page 105) as well as the ski lifts in Megève, Saisies and Arêches does open up a big network of untouched trails, but to really explore the whole area you're better off hooking up with a company that offers van uplifts and guiding such as trailAddiction (**www.trailaddiction.com**). These guys know all the best bits and can take you deeper into the region than the public transport allows.

You'll want IGN map *3532 OT: Massif du Beaufortain*. The area sits about halfway between Grenoble and Geneva, so either is an option if you're flying. If you have a car, it's within easy reach of Megève, Les Saisies and La Clusaz. There's also a handy bus to and from Albertville – you can find a timetable at **tinyurl.com/beaufortain-bus** – search for 'navettes'.

## Grand-Bornand

The small town of Le Grand-Bornand is only 20 minutes' drive from La Clusaz and well worth a visit if you're in the area. It's so close in fact that you can buy a lift pass which covers both resorts. It's not as developed for biking as La Clusaz, but there are some decent big-mountain routes to explore, especially if you head east off the Mont Lachat lift towards the vast peaks of the Aravis.

There's not much in the way of groomed bike runs, so expect rocky and open trails up high that quickly get you into the backcountry and away from the crowds. The lifts take you a long way up (over 2,000 metres), so you can make some big loops into the surrounding valleys without too much leg work.

You can find out more about the area from the general info website: **www.legrandbornand.com**. The lifts run from late June to early September – check the website for more details – and you'll want IGN map *3430 ET: La Clusaz/Grand-Bornand*. The website has links to accommodation too.

# More riding – North-eastern Italy

## Lake Garda

The vast Italian Lake Garda lies just on the southern fringes of the central Alps, but don't be fooled into thinking you won't experience the vertical thrills of the high mountains here, as the huge rocky peaks that surround the lake provide some monstrous singletrack descents.

The area isn't all that popular with UK riders, despite some grandiose claims from local companies that Lake Garda is frequently voted 'the best mountain bike destination in the world.' This impartial poll was probably carried out by the locals upon themselves, but nevertheless there is some truth in the statement, as the lengthy, technical trails that litter the surrounding peaks – particularly at the northern end – are nothing short of world class.

It is possible to hunt down some of these beauties off your own back, either with a fair bit of leg work or by using the lift at Malcesine where you'll be blown away by the magnificent descents from Monte Baldo, such as *Trail 634* that drops almost 2,000 metres back to the lakeside.

However, at nearly 20 Euros per trip this isn't feasible if you're staying for any length of time and it only gives you access to a fraction of what's on offer. A far better option is to book on to one of the many uplift services around Torbole which shuttle to a range of peaks around the northern end of the lake and can offer trail advice as well as guides who'll show you all the secret stuff that's not on the map.

Be warned though, this is no place for those wanting a gentle sightseeing cruise of the Italian lakes. The rocky and steep terrain, particularly on the western side, makes for intense and sometimes quite scary riding, so don't even think about renting the cheapest hardtail option in town.

The best places to stay are in Torbole or Riva del Garda, which host a bike festival at the start of the season – it could be worth timing your trip to coincide with this. This is also where you'll find the uplift companies such as Torbole Bike Shuttle (**www.bikeshuttletorbole.com**) and others offering package guiding holidays – try **www.cycleactive.com**

A good source of local info on riding in the area can be found in the online magazine: **www.lagobiker.it**

The nearest major airport is Milan, which is around 2 hours away by taxi transfer. You'll find many options for travelling to Riva del Garda.

I should also mention there are many German tourists here. I've no idea why this is important, but every other guide to the area seems to dwell on it, so at least I've covered everything.

## Livigno

Hidden in the wild Valtellina valley of north Italy, Livigno is another forgotten destination amongst British riders, despite the stunning array of trails on offer. The area has been given some much-needed publicity through the loopy Nine Knights freeride event and more recently with the Red Bull Wide Open series which takes place on the eastern side of the valley. This is also where you'll find the well-maintained bike park complete with an ex-world cup downhill course, so there's no shortage of gravity competition heritage here.

But don't be put off if 'sick' air time isn't your thing, as the real party piece here is the beautiful flowing singletrack that heads out into the huge remote peaks that surround Livigno. The most epic lines can be found off the Carosello lift on the western side of the valley, although you'll have to climb to reach the big descents which start at over 3,000 metres – so don't try and lug your DH rig up to these.

Of course, if you're loaded there's no need to pedal or push your way to the big mountain routes, because a heli-bike service will take you from the valley floor to pretty much any peak you fancy!

I think that says it all really, in that Livigno has covered everything a biker could wish for in a stunning Alpine setting.

The only real downside – and possibly why it's so rarely visited by riders from the UK – is access. It's an awfully long drive to get here, and the nearest airport (Bergamo or Verona) is the best part of a 4-hour transfer away. If you can stomach that then you should definitely give Livigno a shot, as you won't be disappointed. **www.bikeparklivigno.it** and **www.mtblivigno.eu/en** will help.

The La Bourgeoise spine.

# More riding – Northern Alps
# (near the Grand Massif, Portes du Soleil and Geneva)

## La Bourgeoise

The Portes du Soleil and the Grand Massif offer a huge amount of riding, but it could be argued that the ridgeline separating these two areas is home to the best stuff, especially if lengthy singletracks are what you're after.

The grassy Bourgeoise peak with its magnificent vistas over Mont Blanc lies midway between Samoëns and Morzine and is accessible via the Col de Joux Plane which links the two towns. A 30-minute pedal from the col will bring you to the peak, where two huge descents drop into Samoëns. Either ride straight down the ridge or cut left just below the summit and take a back route into the Forêt de Suet which is nothing short of incredible.

Of course the only problem here is the lack of a ski lift back up to the Joux Plane. Either settle in for a 1.5-hour slog up this famous Tour de France climb or contact us at Bike Alp for guiding, uplifts and accommodation from Samoëns: **www.bike-alp.com**

You won't find much online content on this region, so you'll need IGN *3530 ET: Samoëns* to plan find trails and plan rides.

See Samoëns (page 187) for more information on getting here.

## La Môle and Les Brasses

Driving from Geneva to the Portes du Soleil, you'll pass between the peaks of La Môle and Les Brasses, on either side of the town of St Jeoire. Again these are not lift-accessed, but if you're willing to do some leg work then the rewards are huge. Base yourself at the Lac du Môle near Viuz-en-Sallaz, where you can either climb south towards the Môle or north and up to the Brasses.

The best stuff on the Môle is to be found on the wooded slopes of the western face, where a pedal up the road via St Jean de Tholome will give you access to fast and smooth singletracks that gently wind through the forests and finish in the village of La Tour.

You're looking at a big climb up to the Station des Brasses, but the loamy trail that drops straight down the ridgeline in roller-coaster style is one of the best natural lines you'll find in the Alps.

As hinted at in the first line, Geneva is the nearest airport, and this area is a good spot for a pedally stop off on the journey to the PdS. There's not a lot of information to be found on the web, so your best bet is to grab IGN *3429 ET: Bonneville* and explore.

On top of the world in Métabief.

## The Jura: Le Crozet and Métabief

The Jura mountains (from which the term Jurassic is derived) stretch along the northern side of Lake Geneva and are home to limitless enduro adventures. The terrain here rolls and undulates in a way that the High Alps on the other side of the lake just don't, so you can spend your days exploring the tranquil landscape as opposed to howling in terror. If you don't mind a bit of pedalling, a pretty safe way of finding a decent trail or two is to grab a local IGN map (try IGN *3327 OT*, 3327 *ET* or *3328 OT*) and scan it for the singletrack trails marked by small dots. Pick one you like the look of, find a way to the top of it and you'll find riding that ranges from flowing woodland loam to techy limestone singletrack and worryingly steep plunges.

Nevertheless, we're still talking big height gains here, so if like me your physique is little more – shall we say – cuddly than Bradley Wiggins, you may want to consider heading to Le Crozet or Métabief, which both offer lift-assisted riding in this forgotten mountain chain.

Situated just north-west of Geneva, the Crozet/Lélex ski station runs on weekends and bank holidays in July and August and is so close to the airport that you could feasibly hop straight on your bike out of the plane and ride here.

The lift takes you high above the lake, where you can either pick a line down into the valleys or continue climbing and explore this magnificent, panoramic ridgeline. There are no marked runs here, but it's all the better for it, with cheeky singletracks sneaking off into the woods wherever you look. A glorious mix of loose shale and deep loam means drifting is impossible to resist, and because the landscape is so mellow, you can really get off the brakes, ride like an arse and get away with it. **www.monts-jura.com**

Exploring the vast forests of the Jura.

# More riding – Northern Alps
## (near the Grand Massif, Portes Du Soleil and Geneva)

### The Jura (continued)

Head further north-east into the Jura and you'll find Métabief (around 45 minutes by car from Lausanne). Unlike Le Crozet this is a proper bike park, with marked descents full of berms, rollers and north shore sections. Don't come here expecting an easy ride though – there may be only one lift and 400 metres of vertical to play with, but the terrain is surprisingly steep and full of savage rock gardens, awkward roots and scary drops. Take on the marked black routes in anything but the very driest of conditions and you'll soon see what I'm talking about!

It's not all mental though – the main red line under the lift is a fast, toboggan-style run that really lets you charge, but it's still just too rocky for nervous riders to enjoy. Of course if the park is all too much then there's always the option of using the lift and then following the marked XC trails along the ridgeline to the south with its magnificent views over Lake Geneva and the High Alps. If you want a map, IGN *3426 OT: Mouthe/Métabief* covers the main area.

The major doozy though is that the park has a very long season compared to most French resorts, with lifts running from early May through to the end of September, making this a great spot for a long weekend break, taking advantage of the cheaper pre-season flights to Geneva. **www.tourisme-metabief.com**

Mud is a distant memory above Nice.

# More riding – Southern Alps

## General

As we're only focusing on the central region of the Alps in this book, we're not covering anything further south than Briançon (Serre Chevalier and Montgènevre), but that's not to say there's nothing down there worth riding. The southern portion of the Alps is huge, with big mountains and untouched trails stretching all the way to the Mediterranean, so the scope for riding is massive here too.

Yet it remains an unpopular area amongst UK riders, mostly due to access. If you're driving down then you're looking at a big portion of the holiday spent driving, which isn't ideal if you're coming for a week or long weekend break. You could fly into Grenoble and then head south, but lift-accessed riding is sparse in the summer, with transport limited to airport hire cars – this is why most stay in the central region where accommodation, transport and ski lifts are plentiful.

Arguably one of the easiest and best ways to experience the area is to enter an event or multi-point tour where all the logistics are taken care of. One of the most popular and long running is the Trans-Provence which takes you on a grand tour of individual stages throughout the Maritime Alps which would be very hard to find off your own back: **www.trans-provence.com**

The only standalone areas that have taken off in this region are the Italian coastal destinations of San Remo and Finale Ligure, where you can find riding packages including uplifts, accommodation and guiding, as well as regular flights and transfers from Nice airport. There are plenty of other great riding spots that are worth exploring too though – here are a few of my favourites:

The flowing lines of Sospel.

# More riding – Southern Alps

## Finale Ligure

The Italian coastal resort of Finale Ligure has long been popular with Euro types who see no issue in wearing lycra and body armour at the same time. This is mainly due to the lack of any ski lifts, but an increasing number of shuttle companies and package deals are attracting more and more sun-starved Brits to this year-round enduro hot spot.

The area's roots definitely lie in XC, with ancient stony tracks criss-crossing the hills to offer technical, but gradual climbs and long flowing descents (that have received a fair bit of work from the locals). To be fair though these are proper mountains as opposed to hills, with loamy forests rising up to over 1,000 metres, so full-on DH is possible, especially with the use of shuttle buses, but it could all be tackled on a big trail bike.

A guided trip will offer the best of both worlds, but whatever bike or discipline you choose, you're guaranteed big grins along these sweeping coastal trails that offer fun and flow as opposed to the vertical horror of the High Alps. That's not to say this is a beginners' area though. The terrain gets very rocky as you near the coast, but it's much more accessible and easier going than nearby San Remo. Add to this the perpetually dusty conditions, the shimmering vista of the Mediterranean and the lure of beach, pizza and gelato at the end of every ride and you can see why it's such a popular destination for those of us living in a wet and grey world.

Visit in late autumn when Alpine riding's finished and the UK is a swamp for maximum satisfaction. Get hold of the Italian Kompass map number 642: *Finale Ligure/Manie/Savona* and you shouldn't get lost.

Many companies now offer uplifts, accommodation and airport transfers from Nice. Some good options include Finale Freeride, Just Ride Finale and Mountain bike Lodge: **www.finalefreeride.com**, **www.justridefinale.com** and **www.mountainbikelodge.com**

A cooling dip in the Côte d'Azur awaits.

# More riding – Southern Alps

## Haute Provence

If you're looking for lift-accessed bike parks in the southern Alps, then you'll find most of them near the border between the High Alps and the Haute Provence regions (close to the Lac de Serre-Ponçon).

None of the resorts here are huge, but they boast significant height gains and would form a great multi-point tour if you have your own transport. Les Orres, Pra Loup, Vars and Val d'Allos are within an hour of each other and feature all the berms, drops and north shore that a DH and freeride type could wish for – something that's not easy to come by in the southern Alps.

With 1,000 metres of vertical drop, long descents and some big jumps, Les Orres in particular has everything that you would find in the big resorts further north, but with the bonus of being incredibly dry in comparison. Some might even say it's too dry, with the ultra-sandy conditions making it easy to wash out in tight turns and off camber sections.

Of course the scope for using the lifts and then exploring beyond the park is just as big as any of the areas featured in this book, nowhere more so than Val d'Allos, where massive enduro loops can be made from the top of the Gros Tapy lift at 2,370 metres.

The following websites should give you a few more details: www.valdallos.com/ete, www.praloup.com, tinyurl.com/vars-biking and vtt.lesorres.com

## La Moulière

Situated just off the stunning Route Napoléon around 1.5 hours from Nice, the drive here is almost as good as the riding itself. This mini bike park is set on a sparsely wooded hillside with just one lift in operation, but the loose, rocky descents are a proper challenge for a competent rider and offer the unique experience of riding dry, Mediterranean-style trails with ski lift assistance.

There's also the possibility for some major enduro exploration by taking the lift and then looping the long limestone escarpment and dropping down its south face before returning to Moulière, so there's plenty to keep you occupied for a few days. You won't see another soul in these wild mountains once you leave the park either, so escapism is guaranteed. You'll need IGN maps *3542 ET: Haut Estéron* and *3543 ET: Haute Siagne*.

The lift runs from 1 May, which is largely unheard of in the High Alps. You can find details on the lift, accommodation and the general area at **www.ville-caille.net**

Nice is your closest airport.

# More riding – Southern Alps

## Les Terres Noires

Riding from Digne-les-Bains in the Haute Provence, you'll encounter sandy singletracks that lead you out into the wilderness and into the black lands – France's answer to the Moab slickrock.

You'll need to pedal to access the area, but riding something that you're happy to flick around will let you get the most out of this unique terrain, which feels like a huge freeride zone that's bizarrely smooth and immensely grippy in the dry (which luckily it is most of the time).

Locals have worked some fantastic exposed lines and drops into the rock which give it an ever so slightly Redbull Rampage feel – just without the huge gaps and shameless advertising. Contact Active Azur who can help organize a trip in the area: www.activeazur.com

The downside to the area is that it's a little out of the way if you're planning a trip to the Alps proper. But, sitting due south of Gap and north-east of Nice, you could combine it with the Haute Provence areas to make a great little road trip to some new riding spots. You'll find the tourist office at www.ot-dignelesbains.fr and the trails on IGN map 3340 ET: Digne-les-Bains.

## Nice

This won't be at the top of everyone's list, but the fact that you can ride straight out of the city and into some properly big mountains means you can catch a beach/bike/city break all rolled into one without the need for transport or lengthy transfers. You can head as deep into the mountains as you wish, but one of the best loops is to climb up to the Mont Chauve just to the north of the city. We're talking proper XC misery here, climbing the best part of 1,000 metres from sea level through the town of Saint-Sébastien and up to the peak. The views from the top are incredible, as are the stony and technical trails that drop back down the ridgeline and into the city, where you can find cheeky paths through the gardens all the way to the beach if you look hard enough. One of the best trails, known locally as *Alcatraz*, can be found by heading north behind the fort at the peak and spotting a glorious switchback feast to your left. Pick up the main path along the ridge and follow it back into town.

Alticoop Velo, situated just off the Boulevard Gorbella, has a wealth of local knowledge if you're in the town centre. It also has a description of many local routes on its site: www.alticoopvtt.com. The local map is IGN map *3742 OT: Nice/Menton*.

It should be obvious how you get to Nice, and accommodation isn't likely to be a problem. Check the tourist info website en.nicetourisme.com

## San Remo

Just 45 minutes from Monaco, San Remo is an Italian Riviera resort that could be considered the hardcore version of Finale Ligure. The terrain as you might expect is similar – rocky, dry and fast. But everything's a bit more exaggerated with steeper lines, deeper gullies and bigger, gnarlier rocks that want to eat the appendages of your bike. It's tough riding for sure, but hugely rewarding to a good rider, as is evidenced by the large numbers of pros and manufacturers who flock here to train and test new machinery.

Unlike Finale, the riding here is very much geared towards enduro and DH riding and you'll find few people tottering around on hardtails, with many companies offering shuttle services up the mountain. The best trails are somewhat harder to track down than Finale too, so the guiding services offered by these companies is also recommended.

With all the same beach-side benefits of Finale but even easier to get to from Nice airport, San Remo is a firm favourite amongst European gravity riders looking for year-round action on challenging descents of genuine Alpine proportions.

Guiding and uplifts are highly recommended here, with options including Life Cycle, who can also organise airport transfers: www.life-cycle.eu

## Sospel

Deep in the Maritime Alps lies the idyllic town of Sospel, with rolling wooded slopes that conceal a trail-riding heaven. Many of the local descents can be found on the hills to the north of the town, which you can get to by climbing on a small road signed to Serre de Berrins. From here there are lots of options dropping back into the town and even a DH course with some fairly hefty jumps. But really this area is all about the quality flowing singletrack which litters the surrounding hills. The stony and technical conditions typical of the southern Alps are still prevalent here, but you'll be surprised to find a bit of loam in the woods, which adds a bit of carving and drifting into the mix.

We're not talking massive height gains here so pedalling up isn't out of the question, but if it were me I would head to the area with an uplift option and/or someone that knows the trails well. This way you can experience the full extent of the riding here, even dropping right down to the coast on some exposed trails that seem never-ending. Contact Trans-Provence who run guided holidays in the area: www.trans-provence.com. They've put a lot of effort into opening up the trails and raising the profile of mountain biking in the local villages, so they're worth supporting.

If you fancy doing it yourself then the official site has many routes described in detail for you to follow: www.espace-vtt-sospel.com. It's also got pretty much everything you need on accommodation, bike shops and so forth. As for the Nice area, you'll want IGN map *3742 OT: Nice/Menton*.

The Matterhorn greets you after a long trip from Chamonix on the Haute Route.

# More riding – Switzerland

## Bex

Situated between Martigny and Aigle on the western border is the town of Bex, home to some fantastic, swoopy woodland trails that remain a well-kept secret amongst local riders.

A funicular will take you from Bex up to the resorts of Villars and Gryon, where throughout the summer you can take the Barboleuse and Roc d'Orsay lifts into the high peaks above the valley. There are some beautiful routes to be done up here, especially when passing under the Rochers du Vin from the Chaux lift, but generally this isn't the best high-mountain riding in the area.

The real party piece here is the network of leafy singletracks flowing through the woods between Villars and Bex on the valley floor. You'll easily find marked routes dropping off the plateau and down the main ridgeline through the forest, but keep your eye out because the locals have scratched in some cheeky secret lines that consist of steep drops into long drifting turns through the deep loam. It's great stuff and, due to the relatively low altitude and year-round uplift courtesy of the funicular, can usually be ridden well outside the normal seasons. Head over in late October/November for some fairy-tale woodland carving under the lazy shafts of autumn sunlight that creep through the forest.

You can find a timetable for the Bex–Villars train at: **www.tpc.ch**. For information on the Barboleuse and Roc d'Orsay lifts from Gryon and Villars see here: **www.villars.ch/en**

Bex is one of those irritating places that's right on the edge of several maps. The most useful 1:25,000 National Map is *1285: Les Diablerets*.

# More riding – Switzerland

## Chamonix to Zermatt

A classic point-to-point tour between two of the most famous mountain resorts in the Alps, the Chamonix to Zermatt trip cuts through many of the areas we've covered in the Valais region of Switzerland. The 'Haute Route' which passes through Le Tour, Verbier and Grimentz is a stunning feast of flowing singletracks, forgotten valleys and big mountain views, with a few lifts and buses along the way if you need a helping hand.

It gives a nice little taster of what's on offer in each area you pass through, but consider taking a day off along the way to ride some of the areas we've covered.

Jamie Carr, who pioneered the route with Ride the Alps, suggests exactly that: 'the original route took eight days and allowed for some down time, either playing and exploring the trails under the lifts en route for those inclined to more DH riding, or a rest for tired legs.'

There are many trail options for the route and using a company such as this can help not only with logistics, but in the style of riding you're after. Jamie goes on to say: 'I can take my enduro bike and make the route more freeride by using the lifts more and using harder, more technical trails where possible. Or for more epic "all mountain" riders we have even left the support van behind and done it solo, this keeps costs down but it is harder work. Normally we use a support van and some lifts although there are a couple days where there are no options

for lift use. Even the bigger bikes have to go over the Pas de Lona at almost 2,800 metres under their own steam!'

Contact Jamie at **www.ridethealps.com**

Of course there's nothing stopping you having a crack at this yourself, but be sure to plan each day very carefully, with accommodation, supplies and your general ability in mind! Also be aware that some trails are forbidden to bikes in this area so do some research beforehand. A good place to start is with Gareth at Endless Ride who has kindly written a step by step description of his own take on the route: **www.endoftheride.com/2009/chamonix-to-zermatt**

Tom at publishers Vertebrate also has some hints:

'Rides like this are brilliant. A guided trip guarantees singletrack and easy logistics, but a DIY approach is pretty special.

'There are a few routes, ranging from the 'bike' route, which stays relatively low, to something closer to the walker's route and taking in some seriously high passes with mammoth carries and descents. Get on Google, grab a map and highlighter and look for the dotted footpaths. It'll take five days if you're fit, but adding a couple more might be better. Bear in mind that the train back from Zermatt adds half a day and a chunk of money.'

'Food is easy, with shops and pizza joints in the villages en route, and water from the springs they have everywhere. Sleeping options range from bivvying to 5-star hotels. The former is a proper adventure but means heavy bags, while the latter costs more but improves the riding. See **www.booking.com**

'You'll need lots of maps. There's free online mapping at **www.map.geo.admin.ch**, which is great for planning but rubbish for printing. Otherwise, there's the pricey Swiss National Map series. See **www.swisstopo.ch**

'It's one of the best rides you'll ever do.' **tinyurl.com/haute-bike**

# Eastern Switzerland

The western Valais region is definitely the best area of the country to find that mind-blowing, high-alpine singletrack, but that's not to say there isn't some great riding to be had further east.

Things can be difficult logistically in terms of flights and lengthy transfer times, but there are some exceptions to this, such as Lugano on the Italian border, where you can now fly from London with several airlines. This beautiful lakeside city has numerous lifts dotted around the surrounding mountains where you can gain some height and then set off on some huge and very picturesque XC loops. There are some marked downhill runs from the Alpe Foppa to the north of the city, but really this area is about exploring the rolling terrain as opposed to sessioning runs as you might in the High Alps. If you want to get away from it all for some chilled rather than 'balls out' trail riding then the gentle mountains and Mediterranean climate of Lake Lugano will oblige. The brown-coloured 1:25,000 series of Swiss National Maps should help you out here – you're after number *1353: Lugano*. **www.luganotourism.ch**

From Zurich airport you have the option of other areas such as Davos, which is around 2 hours away by car/minibus transfer or by train. The area benefits from far less severe terrain than the Valais, creating some rolling and extremely fast lines, especially in the bike park which receives far fewer visitors than the big names further west and remains in superb condition. Be warned though – there's a love for north shore here, which is great in the dry and a guaranteed blood bath in the wet.

Outside the park you'll find some typically Swiss treats in the form of technical singletracks and luscious meadows, especially if you're willing to climb on to the various ridges around the valley. This time you want National Map number *1197: Davos*. **www.davos.ch/en.html**

You'll find even more north shore to wipe out on in nearby Laax, as well as fast-rolling stony trails in the woods and a healthy dose of singletrack which can be accessed off the top lifts, especially when connecting between Laax and Flims. National Map *1194: Flims* will get you started. **www.flims.com/en/biken**

# More riding – Switzerland

## Neuchâtel

If air time is your thing then look no further than Neuchâtel – situated on the north side of Lac de Neuchâtel, around 1.5 hours by car from Geneva. The local chaps have created some incredible lines from Chaumont down to the lake with big hits and drops that wouldn't look out of place at a pro freeride event. Nowhere else in the Alps offers descents where you so rarely touch the floor, so needless to say it's not for beginners. Yes there is the option of taking in some XC tours along the Chaumont ridgeline but that's really missing the point of this place – which is to scare the crap out of yourself.

Like many Swiss resorts, the trails are serviced by a funicular which is great because it's open year round, and so is the local hospital thankfully. Have a look at the local site to get an idea of what awaits you: **www.neuchbikepark.ch**

If you don't fancy driving from Geneva then the very punctual Swiss rail system will take you on a pretty journey around the lakes to Neuchâtel centre: **www.sbb.ch**

## Rochers de Naye

An hour's train ride from Geneva brings you to the beautiful city of Montreux, nestled between the mountains and Lake Geneva. The home of jazz is also home to some great riding as it turns out, courtesy of the funicular which grinds its way up to the Rochers de Naye, over 1,500 metres above the lake.

It goes without saying that the views up here are incredible, with panoramic vistas over the High Alps, Lake Geneva and the Jura mountains. Rocky trails snake away in every direction and there's a feeling of endless possibility, which isn't far from the truth if you've got the legs for some big enduro tours which head east into the Swiss mountains before looping back into the Rhône valley.

However the best and most popular routes head straight back down towards the lake, where some spectacular descents can be made back into Montreux. One of the favourites is to drop through the stony switchbacks to the south of the peak towards Sautodoz, before cutting back across the face and then following the wooded valley back to the lakeside via Combarrosse.

Other sweet lines can be found to the north of the main ridgeline above Caux where the locals have been busy adding a few features of their own. These are best accessed by leaving the tram at an earlier stop such as the Col de Jaman.

You won't find anything insane on the trails so you'll have fun up here whatever you're riding, but the long, rocky and tiring descents will be more enjoyable on a burly machine. Forget the DH bike though, as the numerous pedally sections and enduro-style loops mean they're not ideally suited here, despite the big height drops.

Finish with a dip in the lake and beer to watch the sun go down ...

The Biking Spots website has a few route ideas that are worth checking out: **www.bikingspots.ch**. The brown 1:25,000 Swiss National Map *1264: Montreux* will come in handy here.

## Vercorin

On the opposite side of the valley from Crans-Montana lies the small and little-known resort of Vercorin. There are no marked or built trails here, but the huge descent from the Col de Cou known locally as *The Brazilian* is a classic Swiss masterpiece in Alpine singletrack that's well worth checking out if you're in the area.

Take the lift up to the Crêt-du-Midi and then head straight off the back down a small winding trail that drops you on to a firetrack leading up to the Col de Cou. The stony singletrack that winds down through this wild and forgotten valley looks absolutely stunning, and it is, swooping through the wilderness with fantastic flow.

Things get even better as you drop into the forest towards Nax and there's even a bit of loam to get your teeth into as you skirt round the ridge through Mayens de Nax and Dailet. Follow a steep and technical line down to Grône before cruising back along the valley floor to Chalais, where you can take the lift back up to Vercorin.

You can find a description (in French) and map of this route at Biking Spots: **www.bikingspots.ch**. If you want a map, look for National Map *1307: Vissoie* – the area you want is right on the top edge.

High above the border between France and Switzerland.  Photo: Tom Fenton

# More riding – Tour du Mont Blanc

## Tour du Mont Blanc

This famous hiking route that loops around the Mont Blanc massif is becoming increasingly popular to tackle by bike. Leave your full face lid and downhill rig at home though because this is one hardcore XC loop, usually taking four or five days to complete.

The most common and best way to take on the TMB is to start and finish in Chamonix (see Chamonix, page 38, for where to stay, eat and drink), riding anticlockwise around the mountain, crossing into Italy and Switzerland along the way. In this direction you tend to climb on firetrack and descend on singletrack, which is the preferred option for anyone except the most militant XC nutcase.

We are talking big climbs here – up to 2,000 metres per day! But the rewards are worth it, as pristine high-mountain trails soon have you forgetting about those aching limbs, especially when the backdrops are as mind-blowing as this. The descents are fairly smooth and easy going too, so a high technical ability isn't really necessary.

The route is fairly well marked, and although they will need booking in advance, hotels and mountain refuges are easy enough to find. However, there are several variations on the classic route and many choose to do this as part of a guided tour where all the logistics are taken care of. Contact Jamie at Ride the Alps who provides specialised TMB holidays and will make sure that you get round happy and in one piece: www.ridethealps.com

Although you are officially allowed to take this on during the high season, it's probably not a good idea as the high numbers of hikers won't make the trip very pleasant. It's best to aim for June or September when you'll have quieter trails, no snow (hopefully) and a good choice of accommodation.

If you do decide to tackle this on your own, you'll want a couple of IGN maps: *3630 OT: Chamonix* and *3531 ET: St-Gervais*. It might be worth making a note of available bus uplifts if you come unstuck. The reliable PostBus can replace a lot of leg work at Champex (for example) if you're totally destroyed. www.sbb.ch

For itinerary ideas and other useful information, see tinyurl.com/tdmb-info

You can find all the refuges and auberges located along the most popular TMB routes listed at www.montourdumontblanc.com/uk

# Appendix

## General

www.bikingspots.ch – Handy site allowing you to find and view routes uploaded by other riders.

www.wanderland.ch – downloadable routes for biking, walking and, amazingly, rollerblading.

www.singletrackworld.com – biggest biking forum in the UK, handy for pretty much anything to do with biking.

www.mbr.co.uk – similar to Singletrackworld, just a little less busy.

www.pinkbike.com – general biking site with occasional 'destination' articles and great photography.

## Weather

www.chamonix-meteo.com – great for anything in the Mont Blanc region (Grand Massif, PdS, Cham. valley, Geneva, La Thuile, Martigny).

www.snow-forecast.com – individual reports for every ski station (so most of the biking spots too).

## Maps

www.map.geo.admin.ch – free online Swiss mapping. Great for planning, awkward to print.

www.swisstopo.ch – lists all the Swiss National maps.

www.loisirs.ign.fr – all the French IGN maps.

www.istitutogeograficocentrale.it – the Italian IGC maps.

## Accommodation

www.booking.com – accommodation of all shapes and sizes.

www.holidaylettings.co.uk – apartments and chalets for rent.

www.leboncoin.fr – similar to UK free-ads. Where pretty much all the French look for accommodation.

www.iha.com – Another one popular with the French and well worth a look.

Many of the guiding companies also offer accommodation.

## Guiding companies

Hiring a guide guarantees you'll find the best trails. Here are a few people who helped us compile this book:

www.bike-alp.com – Bike Alp (ride with author Steve in Samoëns or anywhere in the Grand Massif).

www.bikevillage.co.uk – Bike Village (Les Arcs area).

www.finalefreeride.com – Finale Freeride (Finale Ligure).

www.mtbverbier.com – MTB Verbier (Verbier, Tour du Mont Blanc).

www.singletracksafari.com – Singletrack Safari (based in the Chamonix Valley).

www.ridethealps.com – Ride the Alps (specialise in point-to-point rides).

www.trailaddiction.com – trailAddiction (Les Arcs and Beaufortain).

# About the author

**Steve Mallett** is the founder and guide of Bike Alp, who run guided mountain bike holidays in the Grand Massif region of the French Alps. Steve is a Trail Cycle Leader and Mountain Bike Leader qualified guide who has ridden extensively throughout the Alpine region since calling it home over ten years ago.

He currently lives with his wife Eleanor in Samoëns, where they run both Bike-Alp and Chalet Sougey, a ski lodge during the winter season.

RIDE WITH THE AUTHOR
**BIKING HOLIDAYS IN SAMOËNS – FRENCH ALPS**
# WWW.BIKE-ALP.COM